Letters Home
MARITIMERS AND THE GREAT WAR, 1914-1918

EDITED BY ROSS HEBB

NIMBUS
PUBLISHING
NIMBUS.CA

Copyright © 2014, Ross Hebb

All rights reserved. No part of this book may be reproduced, stored in a retrieval system or transmitted in any form or by any means without the prior written permission from the publisher, or, in the case of photocopying or other reprographic copying, permission from Access Copyright, 1 Yonge Street, Suite 1900, Toronto, Ontario, M5E 1E5.

Nimbus Publishing Limited
3731 Mackintosh St, Halifax, NS B3K 5A5
(902) 455-4286 nimbus.ca
Printed and bound in Canada

NB1133

Cover photo: Frank Lawlor, Art Kingston, and an unidentified friend.
Design: John van der Woude Designs

Library and Archives Canada Cataloguing in Publication

Letters home (2014)
Letters home : Maritimers and the Great War, 1914–1918
/ edited by Ross Hebb.

Issued in print and electronic formats.
ISBN 978-1-77108-203-7 (pbk.).—ISBN 978-1-77108-204-4 (mobi).—
ISBN 978-1-77108-205-1 (html)

1. Soldiers—Maritime Provinces—Correspondence. 2. Soldiers—Family relationships—Maritime Provinces—History—20th century—Sources. 3. War and families—Maritime Provinces—History—20th century—Sources. 4. World War, 1914-1918—Personal narratives, Canadian. 5. World War, 1914-1918—Maritime Provinces—Sources. I. Hebb, Ross N., editor II. Title. III. Title: Maritimers and the Great War, 1914–1918.
D640.A2L48 2014   940.4'8171   C2014-903182-3
C2014-903183-1

Nimbus Publishing acknowledges the financial support for its publishing activities from the Government of Canada through the Canada Book Fund (CBF) and the Canada Council for the Arts, and from the Province of Nova Scotia through Film & Creative Industries Nova Scotia. We are pleased to work in partnership with Film & Creative Industries Nova Scotia to develop and promote our creative industries for the benefit of all Nova Scotians.

Dedicated to the memory of my great-great uncle:

John Garfield Hebb
born May 6, 1881
Royal Canadian Regiment
(477395)

Killed in the trenches in the Hooge area, Belgium
June 5, 1916

CONTENTS

Preface **vii**
Introduction **xi**
The Letter Writers **xvii**

PART ONE: IN CANADA 1

First Letters Home 2
Adjustment to Military Life 11
The Trip Overseas 16

PART TWO: IN ENGLAND 31

Arrival in England 32
English Training Camps 38
Issues of Identity 46
Impressions of England 51
Leave in England 58
Remembering Life at Home 62
Maritime Battalions Broken Up 68

PART THREE: FRANCE & BELGIUM 73

Finally to the Continent 74
First Time to the Trenches 79
Life at the Front: The Infantry 82
Life at the Front: The Artillery 86
Christmas in the Trenches 92

PART FOUR: THE REALITY OF WAR 95

On the Loss of a Friend 96
Changes and Chances 105
Battles 110
Views on Conscription 118
Nurses 124

PART FIVE: THE END HAS COME 131

The War is Over 132
Waiting to Go Home 139
Last Letter Home 142
Rarest of All—Letters from Home 146

Afterword 153
Biographical Notation on Writers 161
Selected Bibliography 165

PREFACE

The majority of letters contained in this volume are not found in any public library, museum, or archive—they are family treasures. In response to letters to the editor, supportive articles by Alan Cochrane of the *Moncton Times and Transcript,* and CBC Radio interviews, Maritimers contacted me and agreed to share their family heirlooms. As the generation of the Great War has all passed on, these letters are now in the care of their children, grandchildren, and great nieces and nephews. In many cases, the letters were preserved for decades by a child of the veteran or a sibling who perhaps never knew the deceased soldier whose letters they treasured. As fellow Canadians, we owe these individuals a debt of gratitude. They have been responsible for preserving a precious, personal aspect of our nation's past.

The Howard Bulmer letters came to me out of the kindness of Gloria Merrithew and Shirley Ward. George Chapman's letters were shared electronically from Boularderie Center by his grandson Ian Smith. Joyce Crawford of Salisbury shared her uncle Waldo Anderson's letters and showed me his personal effects. Arthur Murray sent me his grandfather Arthur Drake's letters over the internet. Lorraine Coffin, formerly of Stanley, NB, lent me the collection of her uncle Francis L. Morley's letters. The Arthur Harrison CAMC letters were shared by Joy Steeves of Elgin. Bertha Babcock, also of the Elgin area, shared her uncle Leonard Smith's collection of letters and insisted on feeding me her wonderful homemade bread (twice). Mi Cole deserves the credit for sending me her great-great uncle's letters, those of

Arthur Drake in civilian clothes.

William Hape of Ecum Secum. As well as enjoying Kay Wall's gracious hospitality, I was also pleased that she lent me copies of her grandfather's (Harry Heckbert's) letters. Edward E. Jay's letters come compliments of his daughter Wanetta Kneabone, who also showed me her father's memorabilia. Arthur Kingston's letters, written to his sister in Acton, NB, were made available by his niece, Anita Stevenson, presently of Fredericton. Rosemary Boyle of Moncton, great-niece of Frank Lawlor, lent me the collection of letters preserved for decades by her spinster aunt, Clare. The George Loughery collection was shared over cyberspace thanks to Rob Murray and his daughter Cheryl Murray. A typed transcript copy of the extensive and articulate Clarence McCann collection, which now resides at CWM, was given to me by his granddaughter Judith Wile. Another extensive collection, that of Charles McInnes's 149 letters spanning two wars, was lent to me by his granddaughter Jill Clifford. Michael Wallace of Saint John gave me copies of William Muir's collection of letters with permission of Willie's daughter, Marilyn Little of Harvey.

Those letters that are found in public repositories come from similarly varied sources. These include the Art Robinson letters, which appeared in an unnamed Charlottetown newspaper in 1916. As well, there is the large Morell family collection of Great War letters housed at the Provincial Archives of New Brunswick (PANB MC1058), and available online at, of all places, their Irish Database of Letters. Although difficult to find, the several hundred letters from the three brothers, Fred, Herb, and Horace, make for fascinating reading. Twila Buttimer of PANB also graciously sent me a compiled listing of all their Great War–related holdings. Another very articulate man was Duncan Chisholm MacDonald whose large collection of letters is now in Halifax and is quoted courtesy of the Duncan Chisholm MacDonald fonds, Dalhousie University Archives and Special Collections. The very interesting Lockhart collection of letters, including those of brother Lieutenant Frank and sister, nurse Ina, are housed at the Petitcodiac War Museum, where curator Cathy Drury afforded me every courtesy. The Bridgewater Legion, notable for having digitally catalogued all of its holdings, was the source for the Alfred Cook and Fred Boehner letters. Curator Betty Dolliver directed me to the relevant scrapbook compiled and donated by Fred Boehner's nephew, Bruce D. Boehner.

While none of the letters found here originated from any national source, mention must be made of several notable institutions. The Canadian Letters and Images Project of Vancouver Island University deserves credit for seeking, scanning, and posting, on a user-friendly database, letters and images from all conflicts in which Canadians have participated. Their mandate is to borrow the letters and then return them to their owners. Secondly, the Canadian War Museum, (CWM), an institution neglected for decades by successive federal governments, has in recent years obtained a proper building. In a period of cutbacks, this valuable national institution strives admirably to fulfill its mandate. During my visits, staff members Carol Reid and Meredith MacLean were most helpful, informative, and supportive of my research. Finally, mention must be made of Library and Archives Canada (LAC). In recent decades, when funding was neither so sparse nor so precarious as it is today, this institution undertook a project which scanned, digitized, and made available on the internet, the "Attestation" or "sign-up" papers of every Canadian Great War soldier. This undertaking has been a boon to researchers and a gift to all Canadians—the ability to remotely research, find and *see* the sign-up sheets of all First World War soldiers. The proverbial wealth of information respecting each soldier contained on these forms is a wonderful resource. It can only be hoped that both CWM and LAC, rather than being restrained by funding cutbacks will, on the contrary, enjoy increased funding so that similar worthy projects can proceed and develop for the benefit of all Canadians.

Finally, I would be remiss not to mention the support and assistance of my brother, retired history teacher Lynn Eric Hebb, who proofread an early draft of this work. Mention must also be made of two generous grants from the Canon W. A. Morris Scholarship of Halifax which helped defray the initial costs of my research. Their appreciation of this somewhat unorthodox project is a tribute both to the depth of their vision and a testament to their ongoing contributions to Maritime culture and society.

INTRODUCTION

August 2014 marks the 100th anniversary of the outbreak of the First World War, 1914-1918. No corner of Canada, no matter how remote or insignificant, was to remain unaffected by the progress of events which were unleashed on that brilliant summer month 100 years ago. The Maritime provinces of a young Canadian nation were no exception. Not only were we part of the British Empire, but we too anxiously embraced the excitement unleashed by the declaration of war. No city, no mining town, not a single fishing village or farm was to escape untouched and unharmed by the events which followed. Sons, brothers, and fathers left for the army, or became sailors in the Navy, or even joined up to fight in (recently invented) airplanes. Many would not return. Daughters, too, yearned to share in what soon became the great national war effort. Some became nurses and, like their surviving brothers and male friends, returned with horrible memories and scars both visible and invisible to the human eye.

This book is neither another historical account of the First World War nor a dry list of dates and events. The goal is not to catalogue famous generals and politicians and battles. This work is about the Maritimes and the impact and participation of Maritimers in the Great War. Here the interest is in who we were and how we were. My concern is to understand our own past as it was understood and experienced by our people at the time. The goal is not to pass judgment with the advantage of hindsight on the generation of our grandparents and great-grandparents. The quest is to understand what it was like to live in and through those watershed events which helped shape our world. The goal is to read these letters and thereby "to hear," the men and women speak to us across the years. In and through their own words, we learn what it was like to be a coal miner from Cape Breton, a fisherman from PEI, or a logger from New Brunswick, and after six months find ourselves in the trenches of the Ypres Salient in Belgium or in the tunnels leading up to Vimy Ridge on Easter Sunday 1917.

The best means to learn what it was like is to let the men themselves tell us in their own words. Amazingly and thankfully, an extraordinary wealth of letters to home from overseas have survived. These are not love letters to wives or sweethearts but primarily to family: letters written to mothers, fathers, sisters, brothers, cousins, or friends. This in itself is typical of the times and reflective of the way we were. Not only were there strong ties to family members other than spouses, but individuals enjoyed strong, vibrant, and multi-faceted relationships with various immediate and extended family members. Even uncles or cousins were sometimes the recipients of the men's correspondence. However, the majority of the letters found here were written to mothers. While it may be suggested that this simply reflects the fact that mothers were the best caretakers of correspondence, the actual letters suggest otherwise. Mothers were the central figures in early twentieth century Maritime households. Fathers, by contrast, while figures of respect and concern, were clearly more distant, at times even remote. As the letters sometimes make clear, this was often literally the case with a father working off the farm in the woods or elsewhere entirely in an effort to support the family. It was mother and the various children at home, both female and male, often including the young men, who worked and managed the home front—the family farm.

These large families were in turn the key element in the vibrant settlements, villages, and small towns which made up the Maritime provinces in the early decades of the twentieth century. The commonplace existence of these communities, constructed out of these strong families with their love, support, and comfort, is one aspect of Maritime life which has been altered to our deficit over the ensuing century. One indication of this shift is the addresses of the homes to which the men wrote. Places like James River, Gowland Mountain, and Clarendon Station are little known communities and in some instances no longer appear on our maps. Although a few rare diaries (and memoirs written shortly after the war's end) have been passed down to us, the surviving letters constitute the treasures in what follows. The men speak to us in their own words with a vitality, a humility, and a touching innocence which seems to dispel the intervening years which separate us from them.

But the letters need to be read with a certain awareness and sympathy. The very ties which bound the soldiers to their loved ones manifest themselves in a great concern to avoid certain subjects. Letter writers were most careful to avoid anything which might arouse fear or cause undue anxiety. While all letters from the front were subject to censorship, it was not only military regulations which limited content—it was the men themselves. They were willing censors when it came to describing the reality of their situation. Not only did they censor that which was militarily sensitive, but they sought to avoid mention of present or upcoming danger so as to spare the folks at home all undue worry. As time passed, this ruse became less and less effective. Not only was there the arrival in Maritime homes of the official notification telegrams from Ottawa, but the lists of dead, wounded, and missing published in the newspapers dispelled the illusion that their loved ones were, as one soldier phrased it, "just touring" through France or Belgium. However, once wounded and removed to hospital in England, self-censorship relaxed. With distance and the passage of time, the soldiers often let down their guard and revealed glimpses of the stress, the dangers, and the terrors they both participated in and witnessed.

The letters themselves, though a vast treasure trove of detail, personal revelation, and pathos, nonetheless required a measure of categorization and organization for presentation in this book. The following letters are necessarily divided into sections reflecting both geographical and chronological distinctions (signing up, training in Canada, the trip overseas, further training in England, the journey to France). Once on the continent, various realities regarding the pattern and routine of the war common to most soldiers' experiences provide further structure to the material. In short, letters detailing a soldier's first impressions of the front obviously precede his experience of major battles or his reflections on the loss of a friend.

The reader will also note that not all soldiers whose letters appear in this collection were infantrymen. While the 105th Battalion of PEI, the Fighting 26th of New Brunswick, and the famous 25th and 85th Battalions of Nova Scotia are all represented, letters from these men are not the only voices found in this volume. Artillery men are well represented as well, for each Maritime province raised and dispatched numerous artillery batteries during the Great War. Furthermore, as the war progressed, the number of batteries and the relative importance of the artillery increased dramatically. Also included are letters from men serving in CRT (the Canadian Railway Troop Battalions) as well as men and women who served in the CAMC (Canadian Army Medical Corp). In effect, as these letters show, the war was not only fought and experienced from the trenches but from behind the lines as well. The infrastructure required to keep tens of thousands of Canadian infantrymen and artillerymen active at the front required tens of thousands of troops moving food, water, and ammunition forward in their support. To cite one unique example, Canadians were the sole railroad builders for all British Empire forces on the Western Front and as such, built over 4,300 kilometres of railroad in France during the war. By war's end, Canada had thirteen battalions of railroad troops in the field, and as usual, Maritimers were among their ranks.

It is my wish that readers of these letters find them as engaging and interesting as I do. These treasures from our own past allow us to view a time gone by. They allow us a glimpse into the lives, the emotions, and in some small manner, the experiences of a pivotal period of our own Maritime history. These men and women were fellow Maritimers, they walked the same streets and knew many of the same towns, villages, and cities as we do. Not only are we reminded of the way we were, but we also gain a unique perspective on how we became who we are. We learn of the spirit, the courage, and the sacrifice of those who went before us. We see these traits both at the front and at home, where families waited for letters and lived in fear of the dreaded telegram from Ottawa for years on end. Perhaps these letters will help dispel the intervening years and assist us in appreciating the unique privilege of living in this nation. May they aid us in remembering with gratitude the sacrifices which helped shape, safeguard, and bequeath to us this country of Canada.

THE LETTER WRITERS

Fred Boehner from West Lahave, NS
George Chapman from Sydney Mines, NS
Alf Cook from Halifax, NS
William Hape from Ecum Secum, NS
Chisholm MacDonald from James River, NS
Clarence McCann from Windsor, NS

Art Drake from Cornwall, PEI
Harry Heckbert from Summerside, PEI
Earl Jay from Fanning Brook, PEI
Art Robinson from Tryon, PEI

Howard E. Bulmer from Moncton, NB
Art Harrison from Gowland Mountain, NB
Art Kingston from McAdam, NB
Frank Lawlor from Newcastle, NB
Frank Lockhart from Petitcodiac, NB
Ina Lockhart from Petitcodiac, NB
George Loughery from Waterford, NB
Charles McInnes from Moncton, NB
Fred, Herb, and Horace Morell from Newcastle, NB
William Muir from Clarendon Station, NB
Leonard Smith from Grangeville, NB

PART ONE

In Canada

FIRST LETTERS HOME

Enlistment meant separation from loved ones. The following letters are the first ones, or near the first ones, written home after leaving. Clarence McCann, a married man, travelled from Windsor, NS, to Fredericton in order to join the 28th Field Battery. He was not impressed by Fredericton. George Loughery of Waterford, near Sussex, writes from Halifax after joining the 55th Infantry Battalion. Unmarried and similarly young, Willie Muir of Clarendon Station, NB, writes home with obvious excitement detailing his trip to Valcartier Camp in Quebec. Finally, Lieutenant Francis Lawlor of Newcastle, an officer in the 132 Infantry Battalion, writes his sister Annie from Moncton regretting he'll have to miss her upcoming wedding as his outfit is leaving for overseas. All these men, including the married McCann, addressed their correspondence to their mothers. The exception of course was Lawlor, who wrote his sister, but even he mentions that he had previously written his mother. Although writing their mothers is fully understandable given the fact they have just left home, this establishes a pattern of correspondence which would persist among all the men for the duration of the war.

Wartime postcard with a light touch!

Clarence A. McCann
28th Field Battery
Fredericton, NB

March 28, 1915

Dear Father and Mother,

We arrived here safely Tuesday night about eight o'clock after changing cars at Digby for the boat, then at Saint John for Fredericton Junction and at the Junction for this town.

This is a very pretty place in summer but dull now. It seems like a wealthy man's city; there is not enough stores and factories in proportion to the fine houses. There seems to be quite a lot of building going on, but I do not see any crowds going about shopping, although the stores are fixed up fine.

The streets and sidewalks all seem old, being wavy and broken, and the only men I have seen working on them or signs of repair was an old man picking up paper on a pointed cane.

On arrival of our train, Captain McDonald met us and brought us to the Exhibition Building, where they will keep us as they had the 23-24 batteries. It is a large building, and the part we are quartered in is about as large as the drill hall home, but finished inside—all bare beams. When war broke out, they built bunks two tiers high and four lines long.

The night we arrived they gave us three large blankets each and were going to leave us for the night, but we kicked, so they took us down to Lindsey Lunch Rooms and we had a good supper and then back to bed.

Three blankets but hard boards. Oh, so hard. However, we each got a tick* next day about six feet long and three feet wide. First I went poking around and found about a dozen mattresses like ours at home, which I used one of for a couple of days. But they were damp and might be diseased, so I took it back and now use my little tick.

Beach and I bunk together and keep each other warm, for, mind you, it has been cold for a couple of days back. Wind blowing, I

---

* A mattress.

suppose, fifty miles per hour, laden with frost and snow which some wind finds its way in around the windows. We are right under one, on top bunk, but there is no room in the lower ones for clothes or standing room. Last night, we spread our two ticks side by side then threw one blanket over them and hung one over the window where I mean to leave it, so we had four over us.

The grub has been awful, not enough and very poor at that. However, the last three days has been improving until today it was great. Meals—for breakfast: tablespoonful baked beans, small piece bacon, two slices bread, and mug of coffee. Dinner: roasted or baked beef, two potatoes, two slices bread, two carrots or two slices turnip, and cup of tea. Supper: two slices of bread, fried bacon, jam, cup of tea. All in very small quantities, but if we have not enough we can go back for more if there is any left after everyone has been served.

We get no milk or luxuries of any kind. Thursday night they gave us a piece of cheese which the maggots had gone through but would not stay in, and during supper the cook was pasted with cheese for sports. We have four cooks and about 170 men, although they only need 151 men for the battery. Likely they will transfer some somewhere else. We rise at six o'clock, a man roars through like a bull, and if we don't get up the Sergeant-Major comes along and pulls us out. We get up, half dress, and race downstairs for a cold wash with only half enough clothes on, although we have to go outdoors and down a flight of stairs to get there. Wash and come back to our bunks, finish dressing, and fold over ticks and blankets, then at seven o'clock fall in for roll call and one hour's drill. We may go downtown at 5:30 till 10 o'clock and lights out at 10:10.

We are only allowed out between supper and 10 o'clock PM. There is nothing to see except the pictures and twice per week is plenty of that. There are three picture houses here: Gem, Unique, and Gaiety. The Unique had great pictures and the Nelson Trio last week. They are dancers and acrobats—two men and a girl and they were pronounced the best ever seen by the men here.

The men here are mostly clean and good fellows. There are some toughs and bums, but they are generally a light-hearted lot, without much kicking. Some of the men have got some of their clothes, none have them all yet because they are not here or else they have not the sizes. As soon as I can, I will send my clothes home, but as yet I have not got a thing from the government. I may want that bag a while because you dare not lay a thing down. One chap hung a military coat in the dining room and when he went to get it, it was gone. Another lost his puttees from the bunk, so my things would not last five minutes when I was away from my bunk. Few have any toilet articles at all. I had a great shave and wash this a.m., and when I get my change of clothes am going to the YMCA for a good bath. I will tell you about our clothes when I get all of mine. As yet, I have none at all. We fell in with eight Digby men coming over and one (Peck) is a dandy barber so has to work a lot free, gratis.

I will be glad when we start drill as I get tired lying around my bunk all day, but the officers are busy swearing the men in and only got through having them examined. They march about thirty down to the military hospital each day in two squads until done. I do not know how many were refused as there are so many yarns about, but I think I passed alright. I was sworn in last night and the major said he had not the doctor's report on me as yet.

I don't expect any money till the end of the month and he seemed doubtful about me sending money to you when I had a wife, but he sent the card in that way for a trial so I will know about it later. Anyway, it will go to Windsor. He says the government pays its separation allowance direct instead of through the Patriotic Committee as Dr. Martell said. I directed the twenty-five to you as per agreement.

The Ammunition Column have quarters in the regular barracks and are leaving soon, but we do not expect to get in there because the 23-24 batteries were in this place till they went to England. They were here in December and January when very cold and there was no heat so one chap froze his ears in bed. But since that they have put in a furnace and some steam pipes which warm the place. There are about 90 horses which the other men look after from the barracks. There is a trotting park here where they exercise the horses and the stables run between it and these grounds like a fence cut up into box stalls each with a double door so you can open the top for air but still keep the horse in. These are being fatted for England and will leave soon.

We get no drill with horses in the country at all, only hand and foot drill. We have what is called a fatigue party here each day of 12 men who do dishes and sweeping and I served on that party today. We also have a guard of four men and a corporal which is changed every twenty-four hours. Each man has two hours on and six off with a dandy little shack and stove with lots to eat and beds to sleep in. But each man must tramp up and down when it is his turn on, day or night, rain or shine. The sanitary conditions are excellent—good latrine, incinerator, and a man to take the swill each day. A great chance to keep pigs. Our officers are gentlemen: Major Crocker, Captain McDonald, Lieutenant Harding, Sergeant Major Bates, and one other coming, I hear. No non.coms[*] have been appointed yet, although two or three stiffs expect office and are sucking around but don't say much to the men because all they get is sauce.

Several have been taken to the hospital and some have come back; nothing serious, colds mostly. Arthur Smith was ruptured long ago, but I think they are going to pass him after finding out he was never sick.

The public buildings are nice and I will send some cards later. Our crowd is the worse in the bunch to carry on, so there is nothing dull, can hardly get a chance to write. There are about twenty-five guns here (eighteen pounders, I think) which we drag about by hand for drill.

We only use the small part of this building and have to go down to the armories in the town (when we go) for clothes. The livery stables here are only small shacks in alleys and backyards, although there are many fine private houses here. Let me know about the colt home when you write.

---

* Non-commissioned officers

The officers run a canteen here where we can buy milk, pie, drink, tobacco, etc., but I don't spend any money there. I think a little milk in our tea would be better than the sugar they put in it. They cook in large boilers which take two men to lift when filled. There are four dandy ranges made on purpose for this sort of thing, I guess—low, long, and wide with a large oven and tank. We have ten sinks, I think, in a row and if we want hot water we take cold and go to the furnace and turn the steam on it.

We have had no scraps nor trouble of any kind. There are some awfully stupid fellows here who will be put into an awkward squad, I hope, because they spoil all the others. They won't pay attention at all, but when they start to drill us in earnest that will have to stop. This is supposed to be a dry town, but you know how to get liquor in a dozen places if you have no uniform on.

Perhaps Aunt Alice would like to see this letter. I could not write it again, too much work. I wrote Ada*, but not one like this. So let her have it too. Sunday is the best chance to write here, although not much better than any other day. We have two or three South Africa veterans⁺ here.

My clothes are awfully baggy looking from lying around in them, so hope to get my uniform soon. The water was very calm coming over so none of us were sick. Mr. Doering gave us each one dollar the day we left instead of a supper and I have hardly spent that yet. Sometimes an orange or tobacco or pictures is all. I am going to get along on the grub they give us and buy nothing in the food line. We all feel fine and go to each meal with a good appetite and large scramble to get served first. A man needs physic* once in a while on this food though.

Well, I have told you all I can think about, so do not know what I will write about next time. Perhaps something will turn up. I would

---

* Clarence's young wife.
⁺ Men who fought as part of the British Empire in the Boer War of 1899–1902.
* A medicinal agent of purgative effect.

PART ONE : IN CANADA

be glad to hear from any of you as often as you like but do not expect much from me because I do not like that job much.

Yours with love,
Clarence

George W. Loughery
55th Battalion
Halifax, NS

November 28, 1915

Dear Mamma,

I received your letter this morning and that one from Sommerville as well. How is everything in Sussex? Hope the wood isn't all burned. We are putting in a soft time now waiting for our uniforms—all we have to do is eat and sleep. They made up their minds to let us go out in the evenings. The first night we were here we were around with John Adderson—we had a dandy tea at the King Edward. The next night we went out with Frank Dobson, a fellow who boarded in the same house Harold Freeze boarded in at Truro; he took us to a friend's house. He was just going in to get his pen and they made us stay all evening, made fudge and gave us a lunch before we went to barracks. Last night John called for us again and took us to the YMCA. It has a dandy swimming pool, bowling alleys, basketball room, a running track, pool room, band, and everything else that one could want. Soldiers only have to pay six dollars a year or fifty cents a month—I almost think I will join.

Well, I am under arrest for four days, but don't mind that for all in the room are arrested for disorder in barracks, but it don't appear to hurt me much for the captain gave me joy this morning, helping him. It relieves me of all guard duty and I get two dollars extra a month. I don't know what ever made him pick me but I was very glad he did. We passed our exam yesterday morning. Harley and I passed flying, but the other three only passed and come near not doing that. My eyes were the best and I thought they would be the only thing that would stop me. Well, I will write soon again and tell you how I like my job.

Yours truly,

Geo

William A. Muir
Valcartier, Quebec

May 24, 1916

Dear Mother,

So here I am in the field with about five thousand tents and more going up all the time. We had some trip coming up. I tell you I wouldn't take fifty dollars for my trip. We made several stops along the line. There will be about fifty thousand here this summer. We came up around by the Miramichi. There is an awful lot of bog ground below Newcastle but above that it is nearly all farming country. We stopped [at] Sussex for a short time and then at Moncton. We marched around the town for a while then we stopped at Campbellton and marched around town for a while there. We left town at nine o'clock and got here at somewhere about nine tonight, but we made so many stops. There is about four miles of ground as level as a floor with a concrete road run through. The railroad runs within about a mile of here. I just wish you could see this place here; there are tents as

Papa: "Now, aren't you ashamed?"
Daughter: "Yes, of my Papa!"

By 1916 every able-bodied male was supposed to be in khaki.

far as you can hear and see. The time is two hours slower* here than in Saint John.

Well here it is morning again. Our first night under canvas. We had a good night for the first. There is all kinds of amusement here and a river about twenty yards from our tents. We ain't drilling any today. I don't know what our address is yet, but put the same address as usual and Quebec, Valcartier. I have got a lot of letters to write, but I thought I would write to you first. Aunt Jane made me promise that I would write to her next, but there are a lot of girls to write to. I did not see many of the people that I know. But I am glad you was not there for you would've felt sad and it would've made me feel sad too, but I never felt better. There is an awful lot of round about to get here but she is some place! When you get here she is a home. Dow⁺ and I is coming back sometime before we go if we can get money enough saved up. Dow and I is going to try to get together. This place is not as good as Saint John for fun but better for us.

Write soon, from
Willie

Lieutenant Frank J. Lawlor
132nd Overseas Battalion
Sussex, NB

October 18, 1916

Dear Annie*,

Well here it is the 18th and I wrote Mother some time ago and received no answer as yet.

- Willie is alluding to the time zone difference and in his excitement gets it an hour wrong.
+ George Dow Roberts, also of Clarendon Station.
- Frank's sister.

I am very sorry I will not be able to get up for your wedding as we are going to sail on October 28th for overseas, if they do not cancel it again. I want you to draw some of my money out and buy yourself a wedding present. You know best what to get. We had a good trip down in Murray's car. Arrived in Moncton at five o'clock. I went up to McSweeney's store and seen Winnie but was sorry I did not have a chance to see Nell. Did you hear about the officer shooting the man at Moncton? I suppose you did. News is scarce around here; everything is going on the same old way.

We are getting everything packed up for overseas. But I will believe it when I get on board the boat. We have been fooled so often, that I do not take any stock in what anyone says. If we do not go the 28th Reverend Father Murdock* is going. So he was telling me tonight. Well when you have a spare moment answer.

Best regards to all,
Frank

ADJUSTMENT TO MILITARY LIFE

For young men from rural Maritime communities the transition to military life and discipline was clearly a challenge. Fred Boehner was seventeen when he joined up, George Loughery nineteen, and Arthur Kingston twenty-seven. George relates a desertion and both Fred and Art took unauthorized and unscheduled "leaves" before their units shipped out. Art knew enough to get a letter from an authority to cover his actions, but Fred and his friends just took off and later, in England, were punished for their actions. Thankfully, their Canadian officers knew the background of their men and the punishments were not too severe. Moreover, both Fred's and George's

---

* see Frank Murdock's tribute to Frank Lawlor in B. J. Murdock, *The Red Vineyard* (Univ. Press, Glasgow, 1959), 146.

letters make clear the rather relaxed nature of the early days in the military in Canada—picking apples and receiving parcels of perishables from home.

George Loughery,
Wellington Barracks, 55th Battalion
Halifax, NS

December 2, 1915

Dear Mamma,

We haven't got our uniforms yet and I don't know when we will get them. How did my pictures turn out? Tell me how they look the next time you write. How is the wood hanging out? I got a fourteen-page letter from Sussex yesterday, so I know pretty much near all that is going on. I would like to be skating some of these days, but it is very warm here. We never wear our overcoats at all. Wilfred McArthur* deserted the night before last—I guess they are going after him. I have a fine time now and go down to the officers quarters about half past seven in the morning, wake the captain, put on a fire, sweep his room, make his bed, and then sit around in a morris chair and read and do whatever I like. The captain is a dandy man, the brother of Colonel Wetmore, the man that used to drill us in Sussex. I suppose the boys have got to Saint John.

That letter that you sent me was from Herb Bicherton. He says the Sussex boys are all together. Archie left and went to London for three days, they thought he had deserted, but when he came back they left him off. We have to keep pretty straight around here or we go to the clink. I think I will be alright since I got in with the captain. When Harley and I were coming home last night we brought Jack Cole home and saved him from spending a night in the clink.

---

* A. Wilfred McArthur (2303302) of Sussex joined the Canadian Forestry Corp in February 1917.

Well the officers are coming in now, so I will have to go back to barracks. I just had a talk with Bob Long. I can't get lonesome here for we have a little Frenchman here and my sides ache half the time laughing at him; his name is Bill Cormie. Well write soon and tell me all the news.

Geo. Loughery

Fred Boehner
219th Battalion
Aldershot, NS

September 11, 1916

Dear Mother and Father,

This is Monday evening and I am sitting outside our tent. We had an examination today. I was to Hantsport yesterday on an excursion. The train left here quarter to two and got back nine o'clock. We got lots of apples there. I tried to get home last Sunday but could not. I am trying to get home this Sunday. I bought two pictures four feet by one foot—one of the battalion and the other of the brigade. I am going to bring them home with me. It was nice and fine here yesterday. The cake and candy are all gone. One of the fellows in our tent from the Lahave Islands got a box with some heron* and lobsters in it. I am well. Hope you are the same.

The Brigader Borden gave us a speech Friday afternoon and left to go to the front Saturday. Last Thursday evening Evelyn Star [played] on her violin for us in the YMCA. It is getting dark. I can't see. Much love to all, from,

Fred W. Boehner

---

* Likely meant to be herring.

Private F. W. Boehner
B Company, 219 NSHB
Witley Camp, Surrey, England

October 22, 1916

Dear Mother & Father,

This is Sunday afternoon and I am in the YMCA. The country is very pretty around here. We were to church parade this morning. We are living in huts about forty feet long and twenty wide. We have a straw sack and three blankets to sleep on. Some of the 112 from Bridgewater who are at Ramshot* came to see us today. Did you get the violin all right? We are going to get a couple of days pass and I am going to London and Shorncliffe to see Uncle Alf*. The roads around here are fine. We seen an airship the other day. The 100 Batt from out west have two bears here as mascots. We didn't get any punishment for going home.* We had a nice trip over. It is cloudy here today and Mamma, tell Grace I will send her and you a nice handkerchief each. I am pretty well; hope you are getting along all right. Tell Vinnie and Bedford* to write to me soon. Must close. Love to all from,
Fred.

My address is No. 283491 Pte F. W. Boehner
c/o Army Post Office London
Witley Camp Godaling
Surrey, England

- Bramshott
- Alfred Cook, Fred's mother's brother, 111110, joined 6 CMR, June 1915 at Halifax, and later became a sergeant in Fort Gary Horse.
- Fred was wrong for on November 19 he writes home stating that "They stopped me thirteen days pay for going home and most of the fellows in our shack are broke."
- Fred's younger siblings; sister Lavinia born 1907 and brother Bedford born 1909.

Art Kingston, 236th Battalion / Art Kingston and unidentified friend.

Arthur F. Kingston
236th Battalion
Fredericton, NB

May 27, 1917

Dear Sister,

Just a few lines to say I am quite well and hope this finds you all well too. Well when I came back they had me up for offence, but I had the letter that Bill Lawson sent down and I handed that in and next day it was up on orders that us McAdam fellows' pass was good. Tell the 31 wished I had of known you bet I would have took it but I may get off before we go yet, but I don't know, but will try if there is any chance. Got my picture taken and will get them Wednesday night. Got them on postcard. I borrowed a hair sporran* and had them taken with it on. Will send you one when I get them. How is Fred? Has he ever gone jacking⁺ since? When you see Jimmie again ask him how that little girl is. I think she looks kind of saucy. They seem to be pretty spooney• and, oh yes, I got one myself—a pretty nice one too! I haven't got any yet down here. Will write when I get my postcard, so write soon.

    Pte A. F. Kingston

THE TRIP OVERSEAS

The voyage across the Atlantic was a watershed event for all the men. Not only did it drive home the reality of service overseas and highlight the distances involved, but it was as well a journey most never dreamed of ever making. It also brought to the fore family memories of the "old sod." In many instances, an earlier generation had left the Old World never expecting to return. Now their descendants found themselves returning voluntarily, not to settle a wilderness or to carve out a new life, but to fight for God, King, and Empire.

Of these men, McInnes, Drake, and Morell all travelled in the autumn of 1916 when submarines were a threat. Heckbert crossed in the spring of 1918 when unrestricted submarine warfare was at its height and his convoy alone sunk three enemy vessels during the crossing. Drake was seasick and found the food on his vessel rotten. McInnes, while sick for a time, did not complain about the food, while, in contrast, Morell relates how much he enjoyed his steak and potatoes.

---

* A Scottish item of clothing made of animal skin and hair worn on the front of a kilt.
⁺ Deer jacking
• Close and cuddly

McInnes's letter is unique for it is written to his three young daughters, Orlo, Margaret, and Mary—all under ten years of age. Charles McInnes had been in this situation before. In 1902 he had left Halifax for the Boer War, and he had then written his sweetheart; fourteen years later, he writes the same woman who is now his wife and the mother of three lovely girls and an infant son. McInnes is, however, completely New World and Canadian in his outlook. He has no sentimentality for the Old World. His references are thoroughly Canadian—landmarks on the coastline of England remind him of Saint John, New Brunswick, and he remarks that he would much rather be on a family holiday to England than a voyage to war. McInness's pride in being Canadian and his confidence in the Empire's cause is only tempered by his knowledge of what war actually entails. His thoughts while sailing out of sight of Halifax, of home, and of his fellow soldiers, articulate very well what must have gone through the minds of the hundreds of thousands of Canadians who crossed the Atlantic. The pathos of his words speak to us across the years.

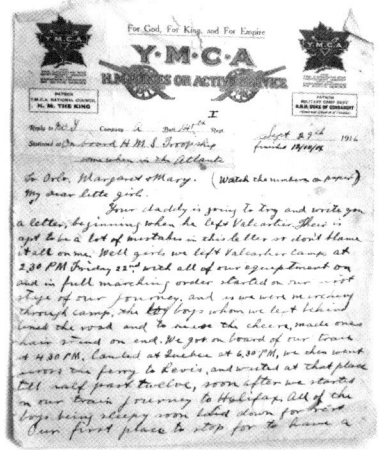

The first page of Charles McInnes's letter to his three daughters.

PART ONE : IN CANADA

Charles McInnes
A Company, 140th Battalion
On Board HMS *Troopship, Somewhere in the Atlantic*

September 29 to October 12, 1916

To Orlo, Margaret and Mary:

My dear little girls,

Your daddy is going to try and write you a letter, beginning when he left Valcartier. There is apt to be a lot of mistakes in this letter, so don't blame it all on me. Well girls we left Valcartier camp at 2:30 PM Friday the 22nd with all of our equipment on and in full marching order started on our first stage of our journey, and as we were marching through camp, the boys who we left behind lined the road and to hear the cheers made one's hair stand on end. We got on board our train at 4:30 PM, and landed at Quebec at 6:30 PM. We then went across the ferry to Levis and waited at that place 'til half past twelve. Soon after we started on our train journey to Halifax. All of the boys being sleepy soon laid down for rest. Our first place to stop for to have a march was Campbellton, where I had a good talk with Uncle Arthur and Aunt Annie. Well our next stop was at Newcastle and they had to take the engines to the shed, for to clean the fires. Our train was in two sections, and the second train caught us at Newcastle, and passed us there...and you know about what time I got in Moncton. I was sorry that I did not go back home, for our train did not get in 'til five o'clock. The trip from Moncton to Halifax was made in good time. We got in there before dinner, had dinner on the train, and had a route march through the principal streets in Halifax. We had to stay in the cars all the day, slept in them that night and 'til Monday afternoon when we had another route march, and when we came back, were told to put all of our equipment out and marched down to the pier, where we had to wait till the boat came in to dock. We waited four hours, went aboard at 8:45 PM, and had tickets given to us to get us our proper places to sleep.

I had a nice stateroom room. There was four of us in the room and it was fine. It was then getting late so went to bed. Tuesday morning woke up and looking out of the porthole I noticed we had gone from the wharf. Asking one of the sailors, he told us we were in Bedford Basin, and stayed there all day Tuesday. Wednesday morning was wakened by the sound of the whistle of the steamer, and looking out I seen we were putting out to sea. A small gunboat in the lead, our troopship next followed by four other troopships. Our escort came about ten miles with us when we were picked up by one cruiser, who kept circling around us all the way over, and our boys had a good chance to see the jack tars, and I can tell you there was a lot of cheering done. It was a fine morning and when looking at the shores of Halifax, and keeping our eyes on the coast as long as we could see land, it made the tears come to my eyes as I thought of all the loved ones I had left behind, perhaps never to see no more in this world, but knowing, that if we should never meet in this world again, that my little girls and baby boy, along with dear mother, would someday meet in heaven where there will be no more parting. And with a heavy heart, went to bed and to try and sleep. I could not stay out at nights on deck for we are not allowed to have any lights. All is darkness for fear some German submarine might see us, sink us, and we would have a poor chance of swimming ashore.

A great honour has been bestowed on Colonel Beer, who has been appointed officer in charge of the ship (our adjutant); our doctor, senior medical officer; Sergeant Major Palmer, ship sergeant major; and poor me, battalion S.M. So you see the 140th still shines. Oh, forgot to mention it before, we have the 136th Battalion* with us and a fine lot of boys they are.

Thursday: Water on all sides, out in the ocean, can't see no land, we see some signaling going on, and when we go down for dinner we find the war news which has been typed out and placed in different parts of the ship where the men can read it. It is starting to get a little

---

* 136 Infantry Battalion from (Durham) Ontario.

PART ONE : IN CANADA

rough, and one of the boys thinks there is not enough air coming in, so he opens the porthole. A big wave strikes the side of the ship, water comes in the porthole, and we have our first salt water bath, but it is with all of our clothes on, thank you, no more baths that way—even our bedding is wet. So much for Thursday.

Friday: A heavy sea is running and lots of wind to make things lively. Some way or other this heavy sea and the boat rocking makes a person feel like staying in bed or sitting down, and the meals don't taste the same as they did. Someone is shouting, "sit down you're rocking the boat," and no wonder, for on looking, all you see is men going to the side of the ship, leaning over, others hadn't had time. What is it? Sea sick! (Oh, my.) I stay on deck most of the day, and when night comes, I go to the cabin, which by the way is first class, and lay down to sleep, one more day gone.

Our ship has dropped into last place. We have the largest gun so have to stay in rear. Well after supper we have a concert. It is being held in the sergeants' dining room, and boys of different units are taking part and it ends at 10 PM with *God Save the King*.

Saturday: The weather is still bad and our ship is rocking badly, but does not seem to rock as bad as the ships ahead. Sometimes you see them and sometimes you don't. More sick boys today and I among the bunch, can't do no work nor drill. We get good news after dinner— Battalion will parade for pay at 2 PM. Sounds good but when we get the amount, two dollars, not enough to buy your wife a new hat (ha, ha). We get war news each day, and when we look at the bulletin we see we are 879 miles from Halifax. A meeting is to be held tonight to arrange for sports. We were supposed to have them this afternoon, but it has been too rough, nothing else to do so I go down to the orderly room, where Sergeant Forrester is giving us some music on the violin (good night shirt).

Sunday: Another wild day, boat is rocking worse than ever. Guess I will stay in bed all day. Steward comes in to make the bed. Darn fool asks me if I'm sick, of course I tell him no, asks me if I want anything to eat (oh, no)—don't feel like eating that's all. I think I will get up and have a shave, but can't keep my feet and can hardly get razor to my face, so I climb back into bed. Supposed to have a church parade, but it is called off on account of the weather. I stay in bed all day but towards evening I muster up enough courage to go on deck, hard work but I get there just the same, but don't stay long (back to bed). They are having a concert, lots of music and singing, but too shaky to stay and listen to it. Two of the other boys who are in the same cabin with me have taken sick, and believe me it is some place, what we are doing to this carpet on the floor. If I vomited as much on mother's carpet I would certainly hear about it.

Monday: Today the wind is more breezier than yesterday, the sea is not so rough as it has been, feel a lot better, am able to eat, but don't hardly know how long it will stay down. Getting our Canadian money changed into English currency and it's some job. Yesterday we went 260 miles, so far we have gone 1,408 miles, leaving about a thousand to go yet.

Tuesday: Today is a holiday in memory of the sailing of the first contingent. The weather is fine, and we are to hold sports this afternoon. The boys appreciate the kindness of Colonel Beers in granting this holiday.* This evening another concert is to be held, the proceeds to go to the sailors'/seaman's orphanage. All enjoyed the concert, the sailors are also taking part, and it has been a grand success.

Wednesday: The sea has calmed down just as still as can be, a change for the better. Can see a steamer a way off but don't know what it is. We are now in the danger zone, and our steamers are taking a zigzag course. Have received orders to have our life belts with us all the time, and under no consideration are we to leave them anywhere. Go up to deck and look over the side of ship watching the spray (phosphorus). It looks like silver, and I get tired of standing so. I take a deck chair over to railing looking at the water, wondering and thinking of you all at home. Someone is speaking to me, telling me it is after 11:30 PM.

---

* The First Canadian Contingent of 33,000 soldiers had sailed overseas two years earlier in the autumn of 1914.

I get up and go to bed, another day gone and an evening of the blues.

Thursday: We are able to see land again, the north coast of Ireland. It is 7:30 AM, and at 10:30 AM not only could see the coast line, but also the mainland. Farms can be seen, also some buildings. I can see plainly the coast guard station. The boys are starting to sing some good old Irish songs, and in this manner are paying their respects to the old sod. We are now passing Rattlin Islands. They are very rocky and hilly, and a wireless station and lighthouse can be seen. I'm wishing it was the coast of Canada instead of Ireland. It is now 11:00 AM. We see smoke in the distance. They are coming upon us fast (what are they? is asked). We soon find out: six torpedo boat destroyers, which have been in hiding (British, of course), are now going to escort us the rest of our trip. They are not a very large boat, but are very powerful. They are all around us (now here, now there), 125 feet in length, and have some powerful guns on board, and also fitted with torpedo tubes. At noon we pass the Giants Causeway. It puts you in mind of the Boers Head on the Saint John River. Its cliffs are very high and rocky. It is a nice sight to see, and the scenery is fine. The troopships are as close together as can be and with the cruiser, torpedo boats, and the trawlers they number about forty. Would make an elegant picture. All the boys are on deck now, shouting to the ones in the other ships. Our cruiser has sighted a ship about ten miles away and has gone to find out what kind of ship it is. There is no danger of being torpedoed or an enemy ship to do us harm now, surrounded as we are with all kinds of crafts. Again we can see the north coast, and with the aid of glasses can see the sheep grazing. The farms are laid out in blocks and surrounded by hedges. I never thought I would see the old sod, and girls, to say that it has been a beautiful sight only puts it mildly. At times we can see the coast of Scotland, but as quite a fog is raising on our port side, the view is cut off. Everyone is enjoying the scenery, some are on the rails, while others [are] on the ropes and ladders—everyone admiring the land. We are still going in a zigzag course. At times we are at the stern of the ship ahead of us, and the next minute ahead of her. We had a medical examination by the

M.O. to find, if any, traces of measles, but there was none to be found. We expect to reach port sometime tonight, but won't dock 'til tomorrow morning. Must go to eat now, will finish this letter as soon as I find time.

We are now in the Mersey River proceeding to Liverpool. Went to bed, but the whistle started blowing so got dressed and went on deck. Have found out what was the matter. Have picked up our pilot, who will take us to our port in safety. Who is the man, woman, or child that is or would be ashamed of the British fleet, to see what care and expense they have gone to to protect us five troopships and the guiding they have done, what must it be to the rest of the Empire. We have now reached the harbour and will dock at 7:00 AM. It has been a very pleasant journey, and as I am writing this, I'm thinking if it was only the family that was with me on a pleasure trip instead of war how I would have enjoyed it. We had a pilot to take us out of the harbour at Halifax. We had a cruiser to pilot us over the sea. We had a pilot to take us to Liverpool—they have all done their duty. And now, dear girls, you Orlo especially, you are old enough to realize right from wrong, you always have been a good girl, take Jesus Christ for your pilot through this life. It will not always be smooth sailing, but if you have Jesus with you, he will guide you, lead you in the right paths, and you will never be sorry for it. Help mother, take good care of your little sisters and brother. I know and realize how hard it is for you, but you are only one; you have a good home, take advantage of it. Learn all you can, so in the days to come, you will be an honor to me and your mother. There is a place in this world for you, start in now, look to Jesus, go to Him with all your trouble, seek his guidance, and he will bring you safely through this world. And now dear girls, Daddy will bring this letter to a close. I will not read it over. I may have skipped some parts, some of the words may be hard to make out. I have been sitting on the floor with five blankets for a table. I guess mother will be able to read it and you know I am not much of a writer so excuse whatever is wrong.

We docked at 7:00 AM this morning, October 5th and will now have to travel all day before we get to our destination. This is our trip

PART ONE : IN CANADA

across the Atlantic, which I am writing today 12-10-16, hoping it may be a little interesting to you all.

And now as I bring this to a close, my prayer is that God may spare us all to meet together again on this earth. If it is to be that we should not, there is one place, and that is heaven. And when you girls, along with mother, get down to say your prayers, remember your Daddy far, far away in a strange land.

God bless you all,
Daddy

Arthur William Drake
Milford, Surrey

October 14, 1916

Dear Charlotte,

Well we have been in England three weeks today and are settled down in comfortable huts with beds to sleep on.

We had a very good voyage over, only two days of rough weather, but our quarters on the boat wasn't fit for pigs to sleep in and the food they gave us was rotten half of the times. I was seasick for six days out of the nine and hadn't anything to eat for four days. I was feeling fine when we landed. There was three other troop ships along with us and the cruiser *Drake* was with us until we got off Ireland and then destroyers came out and took us in.

We landed at five o'clock one evening and went right aboard train and travelled until 3:30 in the morning. We had to walk about three miles into camp and pack our kit which weighed about 100 pounds.

They gave us all seven days leave a week after we landed. I spent half of mine in Scotland and the rest in London. My but this is a beautiful country for scenery, and they grow more crops on one acre here than they can in Canada on ten.

While in Edinburgh I was through the Castle of Edinburgh, also the Holyrood Palace which is used by the King when he visits Scotland. All the furniture used by Mary Queen of Scots is still in her bedroom and all the old paintings are still on the wall. I was also in the Scottish Art Gallery and the museum which contains some of the best work in the world.

While in London, I was through the Tower of London from top to bottom and seen all the old machines they used for tortures in the early days, the axe and block used for beheading and all relics of the early days. While in there they showed us the Crown Jewels. Next was St. Paul's Cathedral and the Westminster Abbey, Parliament Buildings and Museum, but I can't start to tell all you can see in those places. As everything is free for soldiers we are seeing something for nothing, but their prices on all food stuffs are higher than in Canada.

Purdy Scott* was down to see me last Sunday. They had just arrived the day before, but they are going to move to some other camp. I expect to go up and see them tomorrow if all goes well.

We have done very little training since we came here, but our major told us this morning that starting next week we were going to have five weeks very hard training and that we all had to pass our exams in that time. So we may get to France before Christmas which I hope we do as we are all getting tired of training.

Some of our boys are trying to get into the 5th Siege*, but I don't think they will as they left some behind.

Well, I have no more news so will close. Hoping you are all well.

Yours truly,

Arthur

Address: Gunner A. W. Drake
No. 1260329, 62nd Battery, 15th Brigade
Army Post Office, London, England

- Purdy Scott (712598) of Cornwall, PEI, joined the 105 Overseas Battalion in Charlottetown in March 1916.
* The 5th Siege Battery was an artillery unit from PEI. The men hoped to get to France sooner by joining that battery.

PART ONE : IN CANADA

Fred Morell
Halifax, NS
On board Missanabie

October 3, 1916

Dear Mother,

I don't expect this letter will be mailed before we get to England, but I'll write a little every day or so. I hope you get the pin I sent you from Woodstock. We got into Halifax this morning (Tuesday) at about nine o'clock and spent the morning and part of the afternoon at No. 2 pier. This evening we went on board ship and are now at anchor in the harbour. This is the best boat going over. I'm glad we got this one. Howie, Fred and I, and Bert McLean got a room and are to be together for the trip. We had a hard time getting all our parcels and things on board we had so much given to us at the different places. There are so many troops on board that our little bunch of fifty looks so small. We got a compliment on our behaviour and neatness. As soon as we marched into the pier, a major remarked about the fine looking body of men. They also remarked about us in the dining hall. All our men were in full dress, while the others had almost anything on. It makes us feel like being proud of the 65th.

Wednesday: We were up early this morning and had a hot water bath before breakfast. We have great accommodations here. Everything to be had. Two French cruisers just came in the morning. The 132nd band played the Marseillaise as they went by. It sounded good. They replied by raising their flag.

Wednesday 8:00 PM: Just came down off deck. We left Halifax this morning.

Thursday: On deck and strolled around. The 152nd band gave us some music, paraded to lifeboats at 10:00 AM, parade at 11:30 to hear the daily orders, 4:00 PM. At 1:30 had dinner consisting of steak, potatoes, cabbage, bread, and pudding. Parade at 2:30 to lifeboats. The weather is all that can be desired. Nobody seasick yet. The sea isn't rough, but the boat has a big roll to it all the time and the vibration of the engines can always be felt. We are getting used to it now. Two other transports are ahead of us a short distance, following torpedo boat destroyer and a light cruiser (British). We have been in line since leaving Halifax. The other transports are the *Caladonian* and *Saxonian*.

9:00 PM: After supper we went on deck. It is a little colder than it was last night. We had a big time dancing and singing, but after a while the band came out and we listened to the music. We are still rocking along at about ten knots. Howie, Fred, and Bert are writing too. Friday 9 AM: Rose at 6:00 and had a good bath, shaved and hung around until eight o'clock then had breakfast of eggs, herring, bread, and coffee. The wind is cold today and all that can be seen is whitecaps. Everyone has been ordered to wear lifebelts.

Friday 12:00 noon: We have to move our time one half-hour each day to keep up with the time on board. The weather is still good, but the sea is high.

Friday 8:00 PM: We had one parade to our lifeboats today. Watched the 183rd doing physical drill and then came down to the room to read. Read until suppertime. After supper went on deck. Read the daily paper printed on board and found it too chilly to stay on deck so came down to our room and went to bed. Am in bed now.

Saturday 12:00 noon: Got up at seven o'clock and had breakfast. The sea is running high and it is raining and foggy. Last night the 65th did guard. I didn't have to go on guard though. We had physical drill from 10:30 until 11:30 today.

8:30 PM: We had no parades this afternoon. The band played a few waltzes and two steps and we danced for an hour or more, then slept until suppertime. After supper went on deck and walked about for a while. The wind has risen and is blowing a gale. The waves are like mountains, and the ship is rolling and tossing like a cork. A few of the boys are seasick.

Sunday 8:00 PM: We still get up a half an hour earlier every morning to keep up to the time. No parade this morning, but we had a church service at 2:30 this afternoon taking a collection of twenty-eight dollars After supper we played cribbage. It is nearly time for bed. It is raining out now.

Monday 12:00 noon: Nothing unusual happened today. We had our boat drill as usual. Everyone (1,200 in all) on deck and roll called ready for the lifeboats in four and a half minutes from the time the call was blown.

8:00 PM: Fred and Bert are playing cribbage. Howie and I are starting to write. It is raining and rather rough tonight. We are giving a concert tomorrow night. One of the Stewarts is getting it up. Anything to pass the time away.

Tuesday 12:00 noon: It rained a little this morning and it looks like more bad weather. The concert was held last night. They made $84.83 on the thing.

Tuesday 8:00 PM. We had boat drill and physical drill at 3:30 today. The wind is bad, and it is hard to walk on the decks. We have been ordered to show no lights on the decks and no smoking allowed.

Wednesday, October 11, 8:00 PM. At daylight the boats were ordered to speed up and all take their own course going in a zigzag way. All day they have been running all over the ocean. We have to sleep with our clothes on and be ready for our lifeboats at any time. The boats are already swung out.

Thursday, October 12, 12:00 noon We were turned out last night and made to dress and put our heavy boots on. The waves washed right over the decks. I woke up at seven o'clock and we were passing the northwest coast of Ireland. It certainly is a pretty place. The fields and hills are bright green. No wonder they call it the Emerald Isle. It is good to see land after being out for over a week. The cruisers and destroyers are running around us like flies, and the place is crowded with boats and steamers of all kinds. We just passed the Isle of Mann and came within a few hundred yards of that light but never expected to see it. It is a grand piece of work. The big tall stone structure built on a little pile of rocks about a half mile from the shore.

    8:00 PM: We are just outside of Liverpool and expect to land tomorrow and entrain for Shorncliffe. We are not to write for several days, but I'll see if I can't get this off by one of the crew taking a chance. Keep quiet about it. We don't know what our addresses will be, but when we get settled, I will write. I'll close this book now but will send something later.

    Love to all,
    Herb*

Harry Heckbert
17th Canadian Reserve
Bramshott, England

April 29, 1918

    Hello Honey,

    We arrived in England Sunday morning and had quite an exciting trip. The submarines got after us and we sunk three. There was thirteen ships of us and we all arrived all right. I was one of the lifeboat guards, and we were called up twice but we arrived all right.

    This is a queer place—the houses are all brick and very small. We travelled nearly all Sunday night on the train and believe me they go some fast over here.

    The steamer ahead of us sunk one of the German submarines and on arriving at Liverpool the gunner was presented with fifty pounds and a stripe. We can hear the roar of the guns at the front from here quite plain. We had a nice time on the boat. But I think the good

---

* PANB accessed October 10, 2012

times are over now. The grub is bum here—I don't care either if they don't like it, they can scratch it out*. The cars are awful small here and are divided in to little rooms holding eight.

Well sweetheart, I suppose you are worrying quite a lot, but it is no use to worry. We will just have to make the best of it for a while. Be sure and take good care of yourself dear. You don't know how often I think of home and you. We are living in canvas tents now, ten men to a tent. We see an odd airship here. If I ever live to get back I will have a lot to tell you. If you intend to send me anything you ought to send it as soon as you can because we can't tell how long we will be here.

You ought to take good care of your money dear, for when I get back I will be on the bum. I only get two dollars since I enlisted. You want to watch out and get your share of the fish money⁺. I am going to write Fred after I get time and tell him to do things right. Did you get the letter I sent from Halifax? Well sweetheart, the crowd is pretty down-hearted but I ain't awful bad considering it isn't any use to worry now because we are in it and will have to do through like the rest. Well dear, I guess I will have to close for this time. I will write soon again and be sure and write to me soon,

Bye, bye,
Sweetheart
Pte HH 320433

---

* Harry figures the censors will remove this unflattering remark!
⁺ Harry had to leave behind a comparatively nice income when he was conscripted, but he was trying to make sure that his business partner treated his wife fairly.

PART TWO

In England

ARRIVAL IN ENGLAND

Once the vessels docked, the troops, though curious, didn't get to see much. Usually they were marched off the boats, placed in trains, and speedily conveyed across the English countryside to massive training camps. Both Loughery and Kingston were impressed by the speed of the English trains—much faster than in Canada. Although arriving in late autumn, these men commented on the amount of green still to be seen in the English countryside. Clarence McCann's astute eye gives us a glimpse of the workings of Plymouth Harbour, the scale and efficiency of which he found noteworthy. He also relates how terribly the hundreds of horses suffered during the transatlantic journey.

George Loughery
D Company, 55th Battalion
Bramshott Camp, Linhook, Hants, England

November 10, 1915

Dear Mamma,

I just got into camp about three o'clock this morning after a five-day trip. We had smooth traveling every day and we were used good on the boat—although we had very little exercise—only half an hour of physical drill each day. We got into Plymouth about 7:30 Monday evening and lay in harbour over night. We had two torpedo boat destroyers for an escort the last day out, but everything went quiet enough. We started to land about nine o'clock Tuesday morning, and all the battalion except two platoons took trains for camp which was a six-hour trip. The two remaining platoons guarded the luggage until about four o'clock, and then we started for camp and talk about trains going—we fairly flew. We got off at Lynhook station and they said we had to march about two and a half miles to camp, so when we got over the two and a half miles we marched about and it was a good two miles. We are in barracks here, one platoon or about sixty men to a building. We don't know much of the camp yet or how things are going. They say there is over eighty thousand troops. Ray Kerta and George Cuggon are both around here, but I haven't seen them yet. Well, I guess I will have to ring off now, but will write as soon as I see a little more of the place.

Lovingly,
Geo

Clarence A. McCann

June 27, 1915

Dear Father & Mother & wife & Lela & Victor and Everybody:

Well, we are here, but I will tell you from the start. The letter with this tells you up to 30 miles from Saint John so I will start there and tell you as I can remember it.

First, we had the best and calmest trip across that ever was heard of. By the morning of the second day out I took sick and threw up about eight o'clock, then I felt squeamish for four days, but after that I felt like a top and never felt better in my life than I do right now.

The grub on the boat turned out rotten. Porridge and lima beans for breakfast with butter and rank coffee. Soup and roast meat with bread and sun-burned potatoes for dinner. Canned beef, prunes and bread with poor tea for supper. Everything except the bread that was cooked on the ship was rotten. The canned beef was good. Everyone had to be at the table first to get dishes. There were armed guards and Military Police on duty day and night. We were each issued a hammock and two blankets, plate, mug, knife, fork and spoon, and a lifebelt. This all belongs to the ship.

We had boat drill every second day so we would know something in case of accident, but nothing happened. We never got an escort till twenty-four hours before we landed and then a gunboat with speed of thirty-eight miles per hour, and dear knows how much artillery picked us up and took us in. There was so much gambling among the men that all hands landed broke except about half a dozen and one of them had over $500.00 and the others nearly as much. These men ran a game of their own, each for himself and they always win in the end. They all belong to the CPR. I saw one take $95.00 from one of them in half an hour, but he lost it all the next day. I had $4.25 when I landed and have it yet with six shillings that Mr. Muirhead advanced this morning to those who were broke. I told him I was. If you don't look out for yourself here no one else will. You have to watch your stuff like a cat. Our little bunch had the last boat to leave the ship with the captain, so if anything had happened I don't know how we would have fared. We had to wear lifebelts all day the last two days and keep them close at hand at night.

Six horses died coming over and were hoisted up and thrown overboard. Two more were shot. Could not be got up on their feet and had that disease anyway, so were not wanted. The vet who came over is a young fellow from out west somewhere and I don't think much of him, though one man said he had seen him tending horses in camp with his father before. The disease takes them in the head below the eyes. The lower jaw starts at the muzzle and swells till they choke to death from twenty-four to seventy-two hours. Gradually, the head swells, they get weak and dopey looking and have to be put into slings they get so weak. They can't eat and can only suck a little water. The lower lip drops and swells three inches from the teeth. One had pink-eye and distemper with it and he was an awful sight with the bloody matter running from his eyes. He was a fine-looking horse as are most of them and some gained a lot on the trip and none lost any. They felt so glad when they landed that some ran away, although they were on their feet all of the fifteen days. The vet did not seem able to help any sick ones and only used a disinfectant for eyes and distemper. He shot the two horses and made a swell job of the first. I don't think he shot him fair between the eyes and knocked him down. Then after he had thrown the blood all over the place and was tired out, got him right on the second shot, two inches above the eyes.

We saw whales, sharks, porpoises, flying fish, and steamers and ships coming and going and if on a liner with lots of money would be a great trip as would be all of it, and I have not seen the best yet by any means.

We were issued with two blankets and a rubber sheet, water bottle, mess tin, and haversack on Thursday and all hands examined for venereal diseases on Friday. I feel sure we have two cases with us, but I don't know what will be done with them.

We got into Plymouth Harbour Saturday a.m. about seven o'clock and docked about three o'clock. There is a remount depot there of four thousand horses, so I am told, and about seventy-five men came down and unloaded the horses. I forgot, we had to clean all the manure away from those skates everyday and that is an awful job—no room, you know. Once, we took up the floors of wood and washed the steel floor with water. It's all done by moving the horses over one and I was about the only one game to go in around them, so had most of the moving to do. If they did not get over, pull their head over and tie it there, put your back under their flank and fire clear off the floor right into place and you can move any horse that way. Try and see it. You want to do it quick to be effective, though.

Plymouth is next door to Ireland, I guess. Anyway, it's a large city. The docks are all concrete and take the largest liners. A track runs two feet from the edge and on it are four travelling derricks for unloading steamers. The dry docks take the largest liner and everyone has a battleship in for repairs. I suppose there are eight or so of them. The dry dock is very large, full of cars, tracks, machine shops, and all kinds

PART TWO : IN ENGLAND

of shops and cops, too. There are big derricks for unloading coal. They are seventy feet high and swing on a base with a travelling truck on the arm so you can pile a tremendous lot of coal all around one of them. Although we had a pass out, the big mogul, whoever he is, would not let us out of the yard so all we saw was the dock and cars passing the gates. The people jammed all they could to see us, but the cops shut the gates... *[letter continued on page 51]*

Howard E. Bulmer
145th Battalion, Shorncliffe Camp

December 23, 1916

Dear Thomas,

I have not heard from any of the boys since they went across the channel yet. Hazen I guess went to Shoreham, but I don't know whether they will go back to Canada or not—He was turned down on four or five drafts. Great country over here Tom, but I like our winters home just as well. I haven't had any leave yet. Could've had leave when we were over here a little while but wanted at Christmas to go down to Bristol to see Henry Goodall from Cherryfield—you know him. There were only five percent got leave as I missed it for just now. Will get away after first of year. I hear from home and Cherryfield quite often. I sent little Myrtle a card—did she get it? I had intended to write you sooner, but it slipped through my mind.

We have good quarters here and good food. We all had a good trip over on the boat but was glad to hit land. I was not sick at all, but some were pretty sick for a few days. It took us nine days to come over. We had good weather all the way over especially the last day out. The seas were as smooth as a lake. I can't write much about the trip for it may be censored. About the fourth night out it was a little rough. The bunch of us signallers were down below the waterline on the last deck, right up in the bow of the boat—and every time she hit a heavy sea you would think she went down twenty feet. We got into port at night at 11:30 PM. I was sound asleep, but when they dropped anchor it made a devil of a racket believe me. We travelled quite a ways by train, but it was at night and we didn't see much country. There is lots of green stuff out yet here in the fields and gardens.

Well Tom, day after tomorrow is Christmas and we are not doing much of anything. Well I guess I better close…

Howard

Arthur F. Kingston
236th NB *Battalion, McLean Highlanders*
A Company, No. 4 Platoon, Seaford Camp

November 21, 1917

Dear Sister,

*S*uppose you think I am a long time in England. We left Montreal October 30th and was at Halifax a week and left there November 9. Was good half days coming over. We had a good trip. It was not very rough for a godsend. Some of the boys was really sick, but I hung it tough. I feel fine and dandy. We got off the boat about half past eleven o'clock and got right in the train at Liverpool and got to this camp about ten o'clock at night.

You ought to see the trains they have over here. The cars is about the size of a baby carriage and they go to beat hell. I think I would have a great time learning to count the money over here, if I had any. It is quite a lot different from Canada I can tell you. A. Miller* is here

---

• Perhaps Arthur Miller (1102563) born in Caribou, ME, lived in McAdam, NB, joined 257 Battalion January 1917.

somewhere, but I don't know where to find him, but I may run across him one of these days.

It is still nice and warm over here for the wintertime. Suppose it is beginning to look like winter over home now. We are all going to get a pass in a little while, and if we do, I may go to Scotland with Captain McLean. I hope we do for it will be a nice trip. Well, this is about all the lies I can think of. Well, how is everything going around home? Write as soon as you can and often and a few cigs would go alright as I don't care very much for this tobacco over here. And be sure and write often as you can.

L Cpr A. F. Kingston

ENGLISH TRAINING CAMPS

The troops soon became accustomed to the large, flat, wet, English training camps with names like Bramshott, Dibgate, Folkstone, Otterpool, Seaford, and Shorncliffe. Leonard Smith of Grangeville, NB, relates becoming accustomed to the routine of camp life, which included stricter discipline, daily drill, route marches, bayonet practice, and the archaic-sounding musketry practice. The men were introduced as well to other less pleasant realities of military life: lice, mud, and poor food. Mention as well needs to be made of "blacked-out" towns and villages, the infrequency of leave, and the novelty of seeing their first "flying machines." Charles McInnes relates how he saw many men from around home, that is, Kent and Westmorland Counties, who were recovering from wounds received in France and who were almost ready to return to the front. Being wounded in the First World War, unless severely, did not mean a return to Canada, but only a temporary respite in England to recover before returning to the war.

Alfred R. Cook
Dibgate Camp

September 5, 1915

Dear Sarah*,

This is Sunday night and kind of quiet as most of the boys are away to the city, and it just gave me a good chance to write you. The weather here has been lovely up until last week when it turned out clear hell—damn it rained, poured steady for four days and made everything damp. But we were more of the worst of it. Well Sarah, we are getting plenty of drill, lots of road marching, and especially a hell of a lot of bayonet exercise. By Jove if any Germans get in my road I am sure I'll get him first—next week the rifle lecture and range shooting.

Well Sarah, England is a great place, but in a great many respects, it is twenty-five years behind the times. On Wednesday, I had the pleasure of King George and Kitchener and all the staff—it was Canada's review day and there was about eighty thousand Canadian soldiers on the review. It was the greatest sight I ever saw. Sarah, I am sending you one of my collar badges of the 6 CMR* and a couple of buttons and later on I'll send you one of our new maple leaves with the moose head on it. I am feeling fine and do not know what a headache or a swelled head is now. Hoping you fellows are the same. One of the boys of the sixth was killed down in Folkstone by a large motor bus and another severely injured.

I saw Lieutenant Newman today and had nearly a three-hour chat with him. He was more than glad to see me. I meet lots of Halifax fellows up here. Sarah, when you write, let me know about Donnie if there was much racket. So as I don't have much more to tell you, hoping you fellows are well and do not work too hard as you'll get no credit for it. Remember me to everyone, so good night,

Alf

---

* Alfred's sister.
* 6th Canadian Mounted Rifles was organized on March 15, 1915, in Amherst, NS.

Leonard Smith
64th Infantry Battalion, Otterpool Camp

May 12, 1916

Dearest Sister,

Just got yours and Papa's letter tonight that you wrote on the 26th April. Was so glad to know that you got my letters. They will begin to drift in one by one now quite regular I hope. I write once or twice a week or whenever I feel like it. I am busy as the dickens lately. This week I am taking a course in musketry. We NCOs who take courses do so in order to instruct others. We take notes and then get it all plugged in our heads and have to ring it off by the yard to the men.

I got acquainted with a little Spanish girl in London. She's awfully pretty and is quite an artist. I think she took quite a liking to me for she writes me quite often and she sent me a lovely box of chocolates the other day. They lasted about ten minutes in a tent of ten hungry "Tommy Atkins."* I got acquainted with her in a theatre. You know I can never keep my mouth shut when I am next to anyone, not even in church. Will enclose a couple of samples of art.

I am glad that you feel so proud of my promotion. I am trying to do my best with it. If

Leonard Smith's birthday photo for his dad.

---

* A generic term meaning a soldier of the British Empire.

our battalion is not broken up into drafts, I may have the chance of going right to the front as a corporal...

Soldiering in this country is no child's play. Reveille goes at 5:30 AM. That means get up, fold four blankets and a rubber sheet, get washed and shaved and clean boots, belt, buttons, etc, help roll up the side of tent, and get breakfast at 7:00 AM. We fall in at 8:00 for physical drill for one hour, and at 9:00, we change our clothes to drill order and drill or route march until 12:00. At 12:00 we get dinner. At 1:30 PM we fall in for drill and drill or route march until 4:30. Supper call goes at 5:00 PM. First post goes at 8:15 PM. Last Post at 8:45 and lights out at 9:00, when everybody must be in bed and be quiet. We do not get route marching every day and we don't get it twice in one day. Besides this routine we get fatigues and guards squeezed in where our turn comes and an NCO is available for duty at any time.

Must close this note now dearest, lots of love dearest to you and mother and father, your own dear brother,

Leonard

C.S.M. Charles J. McInnes
A Company, 140th Battalion
Caesar's Camp, South Shorncliffe

October 21, 1916

My Dear Girl,

I suppose you are like myself wondering how long it is going to take for mail to reach each other. We have been here for two weeks now and it has been like two months. As I have not heard a word from anyone in Canada or from home. I wrote an account of our trip across to Orlo [his daughter], and put it in two parts making two letters, I hope that she has received it. I also have written four to you so you must have got one at least.

Well we are all feeling better than we did, for the colonel has got us together again as the 140th but do not know for how long it will be. They are trying to make up a New Brunswick division and we will be attached to it. I hope it will be that way. Well we started in at musketry practice a week ago Tuesday and have been at it ever since, even last Sunday we were out to the range all day shooting and did not get back in time to go to church, but thanks, the most of us are done now. I never done as poor at shooting in all my life. We are having a lot of wet weather here now and you talk about over the river being muddy. Well it can't hold a candle to what it is over here. It sticks like the deuce and great stuff to slide in.

I have got a little pay since we arrived here, but it's a hard job trying to make out the right change. I went out to town last night to get something to eat, and I gave them a pound note, but they had me—I couldn't make it out. I had pork chops with potato chips, tomatoes, and two pieces of pie, and they charged me 3 shillings and 6 pence, making a total in our money of 0.84 cents so you see they don't know how to charge. If they had taken all they gave me for pay I wouldn't have minded it at all, for it was the first decent meal I have had since we left the boat. Our mess is simply rotten.

Now we have finished our musketry, I will have a chance of going to visit and expect to go to London next Sunday if possible. We do not know how long we are going to be at this camp, expect to move soon for winter quarters but I expect some of us will be in the trenches before Christmas but am not certain. We NCOs are only appointed provisionally, and they can reduce us any time they see fit and put us back in the ranks. That great piece, what they had in the Moncton papers about Geo McBeath[*] being police sergeant was nothing but a big bluff. Some of the boys in the 104th made it up and sent it over...

---

* George L. McBeath (709550) of 75 Wesley Street in Moncton, who joined the 104th Battalion in Sussex in November 1915.

Well it is now Saturday afternoon and fine at that, so I think I will take a walk out to town to see the sights. You can't see anything at nights as all the blinds in the shops and houses are pulled down and no lights in the streets at all, all is in darkness, so a person cannot judge at nighttime what kind of a place it is. Have not heard of any air raids since we have been here, and as for war news we don't get any at all. As far as we are concerned, all we know is that we are in training, but as for war news there is nothing doing!

Have seen lots of flying machines and dirigibles but none of the German machines. It is a nice sight to see the machines flying around, but they make quite a lot of noise. If you see Freddie tell him he had better wait til he is of age to enlist, as they are turning lots of the boys down for not being old enough and eighteen is too young—must be nineteen past. Have had a lot of our own turned down on that account.

And when I get this suit off I don't think I will ever want to wear one again, not that I am ashamed of it, but getting tired. (Ha, ha.) Have not seen Jimmie Coles* yet, but am meeting a lot of the boys from around home, who have been over to the front, have been wounded and are awaiting their turn to go back. Well as I have till Monday to finish this letter, I think I will go out for a while.

Well I guess I will try and finish this letter. I have been up to the doctor's tent, and I have to go to town to get my teeth fixed. I started this letter in my tent, but am going to try and finish it in the YMCA.

I have not heard anything definite, but it looks as if they were going to send a draft over to France soon, and it is hard to say who they will send. I may be in the crowd. Well pet, it is the same old story over here as it was in Valcartier—no news to write about. The only thing I have now, what I have not had for a long time, is lice, and believe me I have lots of them.

The boys are finding out that soldiering over here is a lot different to what it was in Canada, and that the rations are a lot different, not

---

* Perhaps Birdess Cole (817595) of Rowena, NB, who joined the 140th Battalion in Sussex in January 1916.

as good, and as for butter that is out of the question altogether. Never mind when I get back to that little spot called Moncton I think I will be satisfied to end my days there. I am getting along first rate and doing fine, everything is going along smoothly and having no trouble so far.

They are going to give us a three days pass, so I will be able to see a little of the country. Believe me I will make good use of it. Now whatever you do don't forget a little chewing tobacco. Of course, you know I don't chew very heavy, and with a crowd around it does not take long for a fig to go. John Bradbury* is writing a letter here too and as soon as we get our letters done we are going to town. I don't know what I would give to be home for Sunday. The longer a person is away the more I miss you all. When I go to town I am going to get some cards to send to the youngsters. Tell Orlo to write me a good long letter, and as for Margaret and Mary they can each send me some kisses. Of course, the baby can't do much at present but as time passes he will be able to do the same.

Well dear, I guess I will have to bring this letter to a close, hoping that it will reach you and that I will soon get one from you as I am getting on well. I must close for this time, with love to all, and wishing to be remembered to all. Yours as ever,

C.S.M. C. J. McInnes
A Company, 140th Battalion
Army Post Office,
London, England

---

* Perhaps John T. Bradbury (817890) of Saint John, NB, who joined the 140th Battalion in Saint John in March 1916.

William A. Muir
112 Battalion, Bramshott Camp

November 15, 1916

Dear Mother,

Your very welcome letter received this afternoon and was glad to hear from you. I ain't had a letter from Canada for a long time—only yours. I don't know what is the matter with Maud* and the rest of them. And we ain't seen any one of the boys only what is in our own Battalion—we ain't seen any of the 140th at all, but we seen in the paper that Wheaton was killed. I don't know whether it was Ned or not, but it said Wheaton from Clarendon and Charlie is turned down on account of his eyes. I haven't got any boxes yet since I left Canada, but I don't care about that...

We are getting pretty good grub now, but when we first came over to the 112th we did not get much. But they nearly tore the cookhouse down and then we got better when they found they could not do anything with us but give us more to eat. And one night we had some bread and, as Stella says, it was cooked raw. We commenced to kick and the old major came in the door, and they had it rolled up in balls, and one of the balls hit him in the face. That made him mad, and he said that the bread was alright, but the captain said it was not fit for a dog to eat. And we have been getting better since. We have some wild times here. I was to a meeting Sunday night and was to a prayer meeting last night in the same place about two miles. There were three soldiers with me, two civvies and three ladies and a preacher; that is some crowd. Well this is all. Put B company in place of A.

Willie

---

* William's sister.

ISSUES OF IDENTITY

It is a commonplace to hear phrases like "Canada came of age during the First World War" or that we emerged from the experience self-confident and self-assured, in short, with a new sense of nationhood. The following letters give us a glimpse into this evolving reality. First, there was the sense of belonging to something bigger than a single country, of being a member of the British Empire. This did not, however, entail any longing to be English. Moreover, it was something held in common with others, especially others who have journeyed a long way to fight—it was shared with New Zealanders and Australians. The second aspect of this Canadian identity became most apparent after the Canadian Corps fought and died and emerged victorious at Vimy Ridge in April 1917. It was articulated by both Lawlor of Newcastle and MacDonald of James River, NS—Canada was simply the best; the best country to come from and be in and the country with the best fighting troops in the Empire—hands down! Fred Morell at one point even stated that Canadians would never make great soldiers, they were rather "fighting troops"—men who had voluntarily enlisted to fight and win and then go home again. Wearing the khaki and submitting to military discipline was simply the means whereby this job could be accomplished. Finally, it was McInnes from Moncton, in true Maritime fashion, who mentioned the Sammies or Americans—those late comers to the Great War with which the Canadians shared so much in common.

Howard E. Bulmer
145th Battalion
Shorncliff Camp

December 23, 1916

Dear Thomas,

*I*t's good to be a British-born subject and everyone is proud of the flag which represents liberty and freedom. With also such a powerful navy and army, no one does not doubt victory on our side. The Canadians are treated fine here—everyone is interested in you and will do anything for you. I have seen a lot of New Zealanders and Australians here and they are a fine lot of looking soldiers. Their uniform is nearly like ours, but it is khaki just the same. The Australians wear a soft hat turned up on one side and the New Zealanders wear a soft hat but it doesn't turn up. Well, I guess I better close now as the bugle has blown "cookhouse" and if I write any more I will have to make two letters out of it. Will say goodbye for this time. Your loving brother,

Howard

Address: Private Howard E. Bulmer
No. 832092 11th Reserve
4th CTB, St Martin's Plain
Shorncliffe, England

PART TWO : IN ENGLAND

Lieutenant Frank Lawlor
87th Battalion, France

June 7, 1917

Dear Mother,

Just a line before going to bed. I am feeling fine now and am going out in two days time, or at least Saturday at noon. And am going to the base for a while on light duty. Still address my mail 87th Canadians, France, for they know just where I am stationed.

How is everything going? Gee but the time does fly. Would you really believe it is eight months since I left Canada and pretty near two months since I left England. And the farther you go, the more you think that Canada is the finest country in the world. And every Canadian says the same. That they would not give Canada for the whole of Europe and that means something. For you see some wonderful things over here. But everybody seems more happy in Canada, and it seems freer and easier to get in to the Canadian way.

Well, mother dear, news around here is mighty scarce and there is nothing important going on. And I am anxious to get back to the line again. I have not received any mail for some time, but expect a big one every day.

Well, I must close now and beat it for bed as it is 10:25 PM and lights out at 10:30 PM. Well, as the Englishmen say, cherri O, love to all, write soon, son,

Frank

Lieutenant Frank Lawlor of Newcastle, NB

Chisholm D. MacDonald
5th Siege Battery CEF, *Canadian Convalescent Hospital*
Wokingham, Berkshire, England

October 30, 1917

Dear Margaret,

I wonder how you are getting on these times. The last letter I had from you, you were just starting to teach, and the moving around I have done since has prevented me from hearing anything more from you. I am living in hopes every day though, of a big collection of mail from the battery.

Do you remember the last letter I wrote to you before I got sick? I said then that I had a premonition that they would "carry me back to Blighty" this winter. That didn't take long coming true, did it?

I am not at all sick now, and can walk around the grounds, and go to the dining hall for meals, but I am awfully weak. When I had the measles I was ten times as sick as I was this time, but a few days after I got up, I felt as strong as ever. Now if I walk a little piece I am "all in." I wouldn't advise you to waste much sympathy on me though, for France is an extremely good place to keep away from in the winter, and if I had stayed there I might have got something worse. I don't know if the battery went up to Ypres or not, but I hope they didn't, for that is an awful place to spend the winter in. I see that the Canadians have greatly distinguished themselves up there already. I may be prejudiced, but I believe that the Canadians are by far the best fighters at the front. They have a spirit that carries them through anything. It is not merely in fighting either, for they always come out on top at any schools of instruction, and at any athletic meets. They had a big athletic tournament this summer in the Aldershot Command, which takes in nearly a million men, and representatives from the Canadian camps at Witley and Bramshott took nearly every event on the program.

Last year the Canadians were not regarded as the Australians, who were then living on the reputation they made at Gallipoli, but now the Canadians are regarded as the real supermen (as the Germans call them). You have often read how at the height of their triumph, the Romans always commanded respect wherever they went in foreign countries, well it makes a person feel the same way when he can wear the Maple Leaf nowadays...

So long for now,
Chisholm

Charles McInnes
Canadian Railway Troops

May 2, 1918

My Dear Girl,

Everything is going first rate, and feeling fine. I see by the papers they are still holding the Huns—must be an awful strain on the men. As for us, we are in a very quiet place and very seldom hear the big guns. I see they have some U.S. soldiers in the line now. Was out one night when offensive first started and had a train crew of Americans, will say this much, put Sammies and Canadians together, and they don't give a ___* for anything. No matter how hot a spot it is, or how dangerous...

June 3rd letter

You cannot go anywhere now, but what you see Sammies. I came across a few of them yesterday. The first greeting I got was "Hello Canada, where are you from?" I told him, then he says, "I was down there that way shooting a year ago." Never mind where you meet them, they are always the same. And where you see an American you will

---

* A Baptist man, Charles couldn't bring himself to write out this curse word.

always see a Canadian, doesn't matter if you ever seen them before. Our ways are so much alike...I guess, that is the reason.

IMPRESSIONS OF ENGLAND

England was an entirely new experience for the men, and they did not know exactly what to expect. However, common themes do emerge from their correspondence. The green countryside, neat gardens, fast but oddly designed trains, and women doing men's work. McCann's sharp eye for the engineering details of the railroad beds and the London underground must have made for fascinating reading for his audience. Trains speeding through towns and stations "the size of Truro" also clearly made an impression. By contrast, Willie Muir's innocence as to exactly why the women were doing all the men's work is both touching and revealing. He had not yet realized the far-sweeping effects of the struggle—all the men were off to war! Charles McInnes's letter was written after several months stay, and he relates some oddly English things to his girls at home, things like presents on Boxing Day, children begging in London, and his joy at receiving his parcel full of seasonal goodies, especially his socks, cocoa, and tobacco.

Clarence McCann
28th Field Battery

June 27, 1915

Dear Father and Mother *(continued from page 36)*:

All the houses are built of stone or brick and tiled with slate or iron. Every street or road in England is made of stone in the country and paved or concrete in the cities. Everything is neat and clean as a pin. Though everything in the towns and cities are of stone, yet everyone has his garden and sometimes you would think you were in the country and they are the best gardeners in the world, I guess. Anyway, everything you can see is beautiful and no money or time is spared to make it so, but stone is cheap. We started from Plymouth at ten o'clock Saturday and got to camp at ten o'clock at night and fairly flew all the way.

Now for the railroads. All the roadbed is made of crushed stone, and the rails are of the heaviest steel and laid on wooden ties. All the roads are laid perfectly, curves and all. All switching is done from a tower. One man does it all by levers, no brakeman on top of the trains or throwing switches here. Wherever a train stops there is a dandy station and tower. The tower man throws all switches, even for yard switching, and they seldom have an accident. All the cars and engines are only half the size of the CPR except the passenger coaches. The shunting engines are just like those at Wentworth and pull a deuce of a string of these teapots. They depend on a lot of cars, not what one will hold. The cars are all drawn by a chain and only the passenger cars are connected to the engine with air brakes. Each car has two buffers on each end with a head the size of a tea plate and a spring behind so when the cars meet, the jar is all absorbed and you get a pleasant ride. The main line engines are the same type but larger and a larger tender, but very powerful. No pilot, cylinders out of sight, and no bell and a small shrill whistle. They don't need them.

The cars are made into compartments, seating from five to seven people facing each other, with the door at the side. The top of the door

Clarence McCann

drops down, and there is a closed window each side of the door. The third class is as good as first class, both all nicely upholstered. They lock the doors and average about 55 miles per hour from Plymouth to London, but some places when it is extra good go about 70. We tore through some stations as large as Truro without looking at them and you could not see them anyway, just a flash. The curves in the line are so perfect that the drivers go faster on the curves than they do on the straightway. All the way it was farms and beautiful at that. All the fields are fenced with oak trees or green hedges. Hay and grain cut and going in. There are no big barns except where there are a lot of stock. The hay is stacked as large as a house and the top thatched. When they want any they cut it off with a big knife and so always keep a square face to the weather. Lots of sheep, cattle, horses, and pigs. Only one farm in twenty has an orchard and down where we are, only large fields of hops on poles.

There are no crossings on the railroads here nor a road never goes on the streets of a town or city. When the railroad crosses the rails it either goes over the rails or above them by means of a stone culvert. The lines are all double tracked and a train is going or coming all the time.

Every farmer's property is hedged around so the railway is flanked all the way by hedge and is very beautiful. We came half way to London then our two cars were put on another train and we came to Paddington Station. Here we took the subway train made up of five cars driven by electricity drawn from a centre rail, through a black tube line a funnel just as tight as ever we could go. We left the subway train somewhere near Charring Cross station and got to the street by an elevator. At Charimg Cross station we took the train for here. We went to Shorncliffe but that was two stations too far so the Army Service Corps brought us back here (Otterpool Camp) at ten last night. Folkstone is ten miles away and all these places are summer resorts of fame. We did not know where we would eat, but the Heavy Artillery from Halifax for two days gave us all we want so far and mighty good it was of them, too, but I'll save that 'til next time.

PART TWO : IN ENGLAND

The Column from Fredericton is here*, too, as well as many more with, I suppose, between eight hundred and one thousand horses. It's an awfully big camp and the country all around is camps. The towns are overrun with soldiers. But I only mean to tell you of our trip this time. We are under tents and I like it fine so far. We came right across the south of England and are now only about thirty miles from Dover and fifty from France.

Well I am here safe and sound after thirteen days travelling, (we were on the water twelve). I am surprised at the beauty of the country, the queer looking trains, and their speed and the cheap price of things. You should hear us squabbling over the deuced money. Now it's hard to think of everything, so anything you want to know just ask. After you get this, you will get one every week. Try to let me have news often. Am getting tired writing lying on the boards we have as floors, so will close with my address and love. (I want Ada⁺ to get this).

Clarence

7th Brigade, 2nd Continental CEF
Army Post Office, London, England

William A. Muir
115th Battalion, England

August 1, 1916

Dear Mother,

Well, we landed here safe and sound as you know that we are all well I suppose, by the papers. We had a dandy trip coming down from Valcartier and a better time coming across. There was no one seasick at all, hardly. My head ached at first for a while. There is

---

* 2nd Divisional Ammunition Column, RCAS Corps.
⁺ Clarence's wife.

something for to see when we come to England. You tell the rest of the boys if they knew what there was to see and what a good time [there's to be had] they would enlist tomorrow.

It is pretty hard for anyone to come away from home, but we are no better than the rest of the boys who came over before. The women over here has to do men's work. They have some trains over here. The cars is not as long as ours, and they are portioned off and two seats across them and there is four to a seat.

William A. Muir

Did you get the two cards I sent you? The people are haying over here now and some are getting their grain. This is a great place for sheep raising. The horses ain't up to much by the looks of them. The cows are alright. There is some nice farms over here. I wish you could come over here to see the sights, but when I come back I will be able to tell you all about it. We are going to get paid tomorrow. I guess I am on good now. We are all well and like our new place fine. Did you pay my insurance yet? Try and pay the fifty dollars if you can—I will be as savin' as I can. There is not much to spend money for up here—only in candy. They have an awful time up here with the money, but I am quite well acquainted with it now. I got them to tell me all about it before we got here. The girls here are the same as they are in Canada only they have to do men's work. How is the girls down there making out when I ain't there? Well, I will finish for now. Goodbye from Willie.

Remember me to all the friends around. xxx
Willie

Charles M. McInnes
South Camp, Seaforth

December 31, 1916

My dear children,

This is Sunday and the last day of the old year, and as I did not go to church this morning, I just thought I would sit down and write to dear mother and to you all. I am well but wishing I was able to be home to spend Sunday with you, and would have been awful glad to have been home at Christmas time, to see the nice things that Santa Claus would bring to all of you. I did not see very much of him this year, as Christmas is different here to what it is over home. They do not give their presents at Christmas day, but keep them all for the next day, and they call it boxing day. I was up to London for a few days. It is a big place and there is an awful lot to see. I seen a lot of little girls and boys and I know lots of them are not so happy and so well off as you are at home. You see them going along the streets begging money, and lots of them have nothing to eat, but I know you had a lot to eat, and a good place to sleep.

I was glad to get the box, and I like the scarf, socks, tobacco, oh, I liked everything that was in it. Last night, after the lights went out, we put the teapot on and had a nice lunch. It took the whole can of cocoa. We had toast, sandwiches, sweet cakes, oh, we had a great time. I ate too much, I did not sleep good. We have a lot of soldiers here just now, but a lot are going away tomorrow morning into a new camp. Well Orlo, I was more than pleased to get your school report, and am glad to see that you are getting along so well, and I hope you will be able to keep it up. I hope you are doing as well with your music, and that you are not as lazy as you used to be (ha, ha). I hope that you got some nice Christmas presents this year, and the next pay I get I will send you a few hair ribbons—be a good girl and help mother all you can. Now for Margaret (oh, you kid), I suppose you don't stay home so much, but spend most of your time down at Grandma McInnes's. I hope you are a good girl when you go down and don't make too much noise. I am sorry that Grandpa is not well. I hope that you had a good time at Christmas and that Santa Claus was good to you and that he brought you a lot of nice things. I hear that you go over and help at Grandma Smith's a lot. I hope you are a good girl when you go over there... Now be a good girl, I know it is a hard job for you to be quiet, but be a good little girl as I have told Orlo. I am going to send some ribbons home, and will send some to you.

Now for my baby girl Mary. I would like to have you in my arms right now to rock to sleep, but never mind, Daddy will be home sometime, then we will have a good time. I hope you are helping mother take care of the baby and that you like it. Take care that you don't hurt him, and that when he is asleep you don't make too much noise. I am more than pleased with that mother is going to send me all of your pictures—you don't know how I will like them. I like the ones I have now, and if I don't look out I will have them worn out looking at them. I hope all of you had a Christmas tree, and that you got some nice things. Be a good little girl and take good care of yourself, and give the baby a great big kiss for me. Daddy is always thinking of his family and wishing for the war to stop so that he can get back home again.

Well, I guess I will stop for this time. Hoping you all will get the cards I sent home and will like them. With love to all and lots of kisses from,
Daddy

PART TWO : IN ENGLAND

LEAVE IN ENGLAND

All the soldiers received occasional leave passes from the English training camps. Officers, being fewer in number and higher in rank, were able to get leave more frequently. Everyone headed for London, but Fred Boehner is not unusual, especially for a Nova Scotian, in heading to Edinburgh. As a general practice, all ranks received a week's leave before being sent to France or Belgium.

London was a bustling metropolis unlike anything most of the men had ever seen. Crowded with soldiers from all over the Empire, full of sights to see, food to eat, and beer to drink, London was a place where money went quickly. It was also a city of temptation. Many a Canadian boy had never encountered such friendly women! Moreover, the prostitutes knew that the Canadians were far from home, lonely, looking for excitement, and were better paid than the English Tommies. All these factors made for a potent mix and so, not surprisingly, the STD rate among the Canadian Corps ran at roughly 30 percent.

William A. Muir

August 18, 1916

Dear Mother,

I thought I would write to you again. I have not got any word from you, only one letter that was sent to Valcartier.

We came back from London Wednesday. We had a good time there and the place is well worth seeing. We were to Westminster Abbey to church Sunday morning. We seen all the sights and had a good time. I thought I would be able to send you twenty dollars. I thought I was going to get the money for my clothes, but they ain't going to pay that money til we come back to Canada and we don't get paid here at all. They just give us some money and we have to sign for it on a book and they can tell how much we have coming to us and if anything happens, why, it will be sent to you. We are going to get bank books pretty soon with six months' pay in it and we have to go somewhere and draw so much when payday comes.

I am well and happy as a clam in high water. I wish you and Papa could come over and I would just get a pass for a week and show you London for I know most of the places now that is worthwhile seeing. But I would have to go out to see the girls in the evening as there is so many and no men at all—they are all boys or they are all old men or cripples so us Canadians have boats of them when we go there. I think I will go back again for a while if I can save some money up or if they give me any. I had a letter from Aunt Said since I came across. When you write to Aunt Jessie tell her to tell Belle to write and send me her address. Tell her I wrote and she never answered it at all or maybe she never got it at all. I don't know... I got a nice little girl in London and she says she is coming home with me when I come but I have not told her whether she comes or not yet, nor I don't intend to tell her neither. Is the girls very thick around there this summer?

We moved to a new camp yesterday. We are at Branshott now.
Write soon,
Willie

Lieutenant Frank Lawlor
13th Reserve Battalion, Crowborough

February 14, 1917

Dear Clare and Mother,

Received your most welcome letter three days ago and sure was delighted to hear all the news. Well, I am going up to London soon and will get Doreen something and send it to her. Everything is going on in the same old way. The last time I was up to London I had some time. Lieutenant McLean, our signal officer, and I met two sporty "Janes." His brother gave him a letter of introduction to them and he took me along with him. They both live handy to one another on Edgeware Road. Some place! One of *the* places in London! They sure showed us around while we were there. I never told you it before as I thought it wouldn't be of any interest to you. You should see the letters we get from them. I also got her photo, some girl. You know it's handy to have a nice girl to go around with if you happen to go up alone. Well, I did not tell you what she does. Her and McLean's girl are both stenographers. They only work about four hours a day. Mack and I used to call at office at two and the four of us would go to the Regent Palace for tea and a show at night.

Well so much for the "Janes." There are great talks of the Big Drive. The British have a super tank for every battalion on the western front now and enough artillery putting them wheel to wheel to cover the whole front. There sure is something stirring when they all get going.

I had a letter from Douglas and he said Jack Lawlor* had arrived with his draft. I must drop him a line tonight and tell him to wait and take his leave when I do and I'll show him London. I know a little about it now, enough to find my way around, but if you lived for a hundred years you would never know it all as it is so large.

Well my news is run dry so I'll have to say good night. Love to all, write soon,

Brother, Frank

---

* Lieutenant John L. Lawlor, born July 30, 1894, of Newcastle, NB, who joined the draft of 12th Artillery Battery September 2, 1916.

Private Fred Boehner
Witley
17th Reserve Battalion

January 20, 1918

Dear Mother and Father,

This is Sunday evening and I am in the recreation room. I was on church parade as usual this morning and this afternoon I cleaned up well. I had my pass at last so I went up to Edinburgh. I had a fine time. I was with a fellow out of our section by the name of Fraser. The air was fine and bracing and I felt great. I had a skate while I was up there, but oh! what skates I had. They couldn't have been sharpened for a year and every stroke I took they would slide off about a yard. I was through the castle and the palace. They are great old places. I wish you could see them. I am sending you some photos of the place next week.

I received two of your boxes on Wednesday with dates, cakes, fudge, and canned ham in them. Everything was fine, especially, tell Grace*, the fudge. Also, I received the box yesterday with the present from Aunt Sophie in it. Please thank her for me for the gloves, tell her they are fine and warm and so nice and soft. Please tell Grace to send me a photo of Vinnie and Bedford⁺ skating.

Well we are having rather wet weather here; it snows one day and rains the next. Did I tell you I received the cable for five pounds all right? I needed it to go on pass with. I am feeling fine and hope you are the same. Are there very many fellows being called up by the conscription around home? You very seldom see a man of military age walking around over here. I am thinking of getting some photos taken of myself soon to send to you. I received your letters written the 17th of December and also Grace's of the 19th with the PO order in it.

---

* Fred's older sister, born 1898.
⁺ Fred's younger siblings; sister Lavinia born 1907 and brother Bedford born 1909.

PART TWO : IN ENGLAND

Please thank Mr. Heckman* for the letter he sent to me and tell him I was so pleased to hear from him. I forgot to tell you about the lobsters—well they didn't last long. Hope you will be able to get more men to work for you. This letter is getting very long for me to write, so I shall have to close. Love to all from,

Fred

REMEMBERING LIFE AT HOME

For most of the young men enlisted life was their first extended stay away from home. Once the excitement and bravado wore off, their thoughts naturally turned to the homes and families they left behind. Willie Muir was frustrated at not having received any letters from home as yet and threatened his mother not to write as often—a threat he was to repeat but didn't and couldn't follow through on. Willie's youth shines through when he wonders if the girls at home are asking about him. His main concern, however, is life at home: the oats in the field he harrowed last spring, whether the haying is finished, or if there are any moose or deer about and who will be lumbering in the woods the coming winter. Francis Morley, an Albertan, has similar concerns in the letter to his sister. Art Harrison, who joined No. VIII Overseas Field Ambulance at Saint John, relates how many of the local 104th Infantry Battalion boys he has seen lately and wishes he was home to pick blueberries. Ed Jay's letter is unique for it reveals his interest and concern not for the farm but for its people, in this case, his fourteen-year-old sister, Helen. He tells her the big news which will make her ears tingle—he has a girl in Scotland. One can easily imagine her excitement at the news and the revelation that Edward's girl calls him neither Eddie or Edward but "Teddie." How Helen must have relished sharing this news! Such thoughtfulness from a man serving in France with the famed "Fighting 26th" just a few months after Vimy reveals much about the nature and qualities of this particular Maritimer.

---

*An employee of the Boehners who boarded with the family.

William A. Muir
115th Battalion, Bramshott

September 6, 1916

Dear Mother,

I received your letter and was glad to hear from you. The reason that I sent three cards—they were all that we were allowed to write then and we did not have to put any stamps on them neither and it takes a long time for mail to get around. It has to go to the army post office and all around before we get it and the same the way going from here. It only takes 5–6 days to go across but the boats stays in the dock 4–5 days and sometimes more to get their cargo to come back and the same on this side. The letter that you sent was dated on the 18th and it was the 5th when I got it. So you see that is over three weeks to get from one person to another on the other side of the pond.

You tell me to write often. I think I wrote every week since I came over here to you folks and that is plenty often. When I go to France I don't think I will bother writing to any one at all, but I suppose I will have to write to you once in a while to show there is no hard feeling.

Milly Hoyt seemed pretty anxious about me...Is she the only one that is anxious about me? Doesn't Annie Kirkkiren mention me at all? I sent a flag in Aunt Jessie's letter—I forgot to put it in yours so I told her to give it to you for a souvenir of this place. It don't amount to much.

Is Samuel going in lumbering this winter? Have any one got any deer or moose around there yet this fall? Is the chickens very thick or they miserable like they was last fall? Have you got that rifle up there yet? I wish I was back for a week or two to hunt and fish and sport. Robert Wheaton[*] is going to try to come over and see us before we go

---

[*] Robert W. Wheaton (445203) born 1896 at Clarendon, NB, who joined the 55 Infantry Battalion at Sussex in July 1915.

to France. Although we don't go to the trenches just as soon as we get there. We have to drill there for a while and there is an awful lot there now and they will have to go ahead of us.

The weather is very wet over here and damp and cold at night. We are getting along fine now—supposing we do get wet. There must have been a great crop of hay on the place this year to what it was last year. We put it all over the cows and had the hay for wild hay and straw. Are you cutting any other hay besides the lower field or will that be enough with the straw? How is the oats in the new land that I dug up with the harrow last spring? I suspect them down in the new broke ground is pretty good, ain't they? I suppose you will be all done haying and harrowing too when this gets there. How many cord of wood do you expect to have this year? What is it? Mostly poplar, spruce? I suppose the girls will more than fly now since Herb has got his colt. He must have a nice young team now...What is the old man doing? Is Millie Hazen asking about me? You tell her to write to me and I will answer it for there ain't much else to do here. Write soon.

William Muir

Arthur Harrison
Canadian Army Medical Corps, Kitchener Hospital

June 1, 1917

Dear Mother,

*Y*our letter was gladly received...Oh say, as I was walking down town last night I bumped right into Ora Steeves*, John Smith⁺,

---

* Ora Steeves (709175) from Elgin, NB, who joined the 104 Battalion at Sussex on September 24, 1915.

⁺ Possibly Joseph Smith (709142) from Hopewell Hill, NB, who joined the 104 Battalion at Sussex on September 24, 1915.

and another fellow from home. Some surprise they gave me too. Gee! But they have failed, especially Ora (he is just like a shadow). Now they are stationed at Shoreham not far from here and are coming up this afternoon. They say Manning Douthright* is out there too.

How much money have you received from my assignment? You must have now about a hundred dollars. What are you doing with it?

Well two days have elapsed since I started this letter. Today is the 3rd and today the sun is beating down upon this little hut which is covered with corrugated steel shingles. Which makes it very hot, but nevertheless I am going to finish this letter regardless of the heat.

Did I tell you about moving down to the surgical huts? I moved some time ago, it is a better place for me as there is more air (and not so much to do). Are there any blueberries this summer? How I should like to go out on the plains and have my feed. I suppose you are making hay to beat sixty now!

Art Harrison. Note the Red Cross on his uniform.

What kind of Sunday school organization have you got? Who is superintendent? Well, I will have to close as it is rather too hot for writing in this tin shack today. So good day.

Your affectionate son,
Arthur

- Possibly Clifford Douthwright (709366) from Riverside, NB, who joined the 104 Battalion at Sussex on September 24, 1915.

Edward Earl Jay
26th Battalion, Somewhere in France

July 15, 1917

My dear sister,

This evening I send you a few lines to say I am still well and happy, hope you are all the same. Now my dear little Helen, I am going to say something in this letter that will please "Has" "hum."* Well, while I was on furlough last fall I got acquainted with a very nice little girl in Edinburgh. We have both been writing to each other every week since I saw her last and that was about the middle of December 1916. She is a very nice, kind girl, also really pretty but small. She is about the same size as *Ellen* but about twenty-five times as nice looking. She's nineteen years of age, she has sent me parcels, also many nice encouraging letters that helps to keep one up quite a lot. Her name and address is Bella Gillies, 176 Easter Road, Edinburgh, Scotland. But what do you know: the two mayflowers you sent me, I got them OK and I sent them both to Bella. One for her and the other to keep for 'til later, so when going to Canada I will take it back for the round trip. I said they came from you, so today I received a letter from my own Bella asking for your address as she is going to send you a remembrance of Scotland. So Helen dear, if you happen to receive anything from her please write her a very nice note in thanking her for she has a good education and nice too. I know you will, won't you? If you don't you will hurt my feelings, for she has been too nice and kind to Ted when far from home to act any other way but nice with her. When I was on furlough she used me like a brother and that is the part that made me admire her. And if all goes the way I hope it will, she will see PEI with Ted's return.

How is everybody around? I hope everything is going good down home. Now dear sister I really don't know what my love is going to

---

* Probably a nickname for his little sister, perhaps his rendering of her first attempts to articulate her own name: "hashum" for Helen.

send you at all, but expect she will tell me in her next letter. She never puts Eddie or Edward in her letters, it is always Teddie. Now I guess I will close as I have no news to write at all, so sending my best regards to all around and love and kisses to all at home. I remain,
your big brother,
Teddie

Don't worry if you don't hear from me every week. I will do my best in writing.

Francis L. Morley
50th Battalion, France

October 7, 1917

Dear Sister,

Will try and answer your welcome letter that I received some time ago. I am sorry that you had to go home so soon. I hope Harry [her husband] is all right now. How long will it be before he is able to attend to his business again?

I guess mother was very disappointed on account of losing you so soon. I guess the farmers will be threshing out there now. How are the crops turning out? I got my first letter from Jack the other day—he was in eastern Canada. He had a time I guess crossing the pond... We are having some wet weather at present. What condition is things in out at home? Is mother having a hard time of it? I don't want her to stay out there alone this winter. It will be too much on her to do it. She has done great as it is.

Yes, I think it is better to send the mail right to France...

Well, I guess I will close for this time, write soon,
Your brother,
Bill

ℳARITIME 𝓑ATTALIONS 𝓑ROKEN UP

Recruitment was conducted locally and depended for success upon local, regional, and provincial pride, patriotism and the ties of family and friends. To use New Brunswick as an example, Charles McInnes's infantry battalion was the 140th which was mobilized at Saint John in late 1915 and early 1916. At roughly the same time, the 104th Battalion was mobilized at Sussex, the 145th Battalion was being recruited almost exclusively from Kent and Westmorland Counties and Frank Lawlor's 132nd Battalion was being raised with men from northern New Brunswick. Earlier, in the summer of 1915, the 55th Battalion had been filled with men from throughout New Brunswick and PEI. Unlike the earlier battalions, the 25th from Nova Scotia and the 26th from New Brunswick, both of which were recruited in the autumn of 1914, none of these infantry battalions made it to the front intact. Due to high casualty rates, all the men were needed as reinforcements for battalions already serving at the front. This was also true for all the infantry battalions raised at this period and later in both PEI and Nova Scotia, except for the 85th of Nova Scotia.

The following letters reveal the shock, disappointment, and even disillusionment and bitterness felt at the break up of these proud Maritime battalions. We also gain a glimpse of what the rank and file thought of certain of their former officers who, in some instances, secured "bomb-proof" jobs well behind the lines. Not all officers did so and Frank Lawlor represents a sizeable group who, after their battalion was broken up for reinforcements, actively sought out placement with another infantry battalion so he could serve at the front.

Charles McInnes
140th Battalion, Caesar's Camp

October 9, 1916

My dear Niece,

I am going to try and write a few lines today. This is the first time I have had time, you may say, to myself, since I arrived. I am feeling first rate but disappointed. We were just two weeks from the time we left Valcartier till we arrived here, and had a first rate trip of it and everything went along as smoothly as possible.

We arrived here last Friday afternoon, had an inspection and before we knew where we were at were disbanded as a battalion and two of the companies were handed over to the RCR. The companies were A and C; B and D were handed over to the Princess Pats. We could not have got into any two better battalions. We are awful sorry that we are not to be known as 140th, but I suppose it can't be helped. We don't even know who our officers are, or if we will have our old ones or not. I am still holding my rank, but do not know how long I will be able to hold it.

We are camped just outside of Folkstone, a place of about forty thousand population, they say, and it is a fine place. We are only eight miles from Dover, and they say on a good still night you can hear the guns roaring. Have seen a lot of airships, but none of the Kaiser's so far. This place has not been bombarded as yet, but

Company Sergeant Major Charles McInnes.

PART TWO : IN ENGLAND

everything is in darkness at night. This is a Canadian camp, but the troops are scattered all over it. The 104th are camped here with us, and a lot of wounded soldiers are around. The 145th are about two miles from us, as they have been broken up also, do not know what battalion they are with, have seen a number of the boys from home including Art Fergusson and Midget Gibson, both are looking first rate. They were in the 55th, but have not been over to France yet. There are a lot of the other boys here—I have seen all of the boys of the 104th from home and to start and name them would take a lot of paper, but all are feeling first rate and anxious to get over to France.

I intended to go to church last night but was not able to go, but if here next Sunday, intend to go if possible. We have had some of our men turned down since we got here, but there is going to be another examination. I am finding it hard to write this letter, as I am laying on my stomach on the floor, the paper in a kit bag, have not got my own tent yet, but will have tonight. It was a nice trip coming around the north of Ireland. Had six torpedo destroyers to escort us and landed at Liverpool, and the scenery was fine. Would like to have money enough to travel all through the place.

Well, I started this letter early this morning and it is now twelve noon, and if I have to go out soon, hard to tell when I will get it finished. I did not have to go out on parade but have got enough work around here to keep me busy. There is no news to write about here but will try and make the next letter a little more interesting. Hoping that the youngsters are all well and that the folks are in good health. I suppose all are like myself, lonesome, and all wishing we were together. Never mind pet, everything will come out OK. The colonel has gone to London to see if he can do something for us. I hope he will succeed; we will know in a day or two. Have not got the youngster's letter done yet but will try and get it away on next boat. Well, as this is all I can think about this morning, will close. With love to all, yours ever,

C.

William Muir
B Company, 115th Battalion
Bramshott Camp

October 22, 1916

Dear Mother,

I just thought I would write you a line to let you know that I am alive yet and having a good time. I got a letter from you last week and answered it and thought I would write again. Our battalion has been all broken up and all the boys have been transferred to the 112 Battalion*, but me and Rankin and Mel are still in the old 115, but don't know where we are going, but we are trying to get up with the rest. They are all out of the 115, but about 130 or so and they are going somewhere soon. It is raining here tonight and I am on guard from two 'til six in the morning. Old Colonel Widderburn's warriors are pretty well scattered out now. The boys say he has got a good job going 'round and shaking hands with the boys and crying. Well that is a pretty good job if he keeps safer but if he gets boot he won't be able to cry.

Well, this is all the news for this time. Aunt Said said that she had started a box for Christmas to me when I got her last letter. I got it the same time as your last one. Well, I don't know what my address will be but use the same old one til you hear from me again. Soldiering is a good life but it ain't much when you get all broke up this way and don't know where you are going to get your next meal, but it can't be helped so I will pack all my troubles in my old kit bag and smile. If they put me in some other battalion I will stay there. It won't take long to get acquainted and I will have a good a time there

---

* 112 Nova Scotia Battalion—it too was broken up for reinforcements.

as anywheres else. But I think I will get up with the rest of the boys. This is all for now, so goodbye from your loving boy,

 Willie—write soon

Lieutenant Frank Lawlor
87th Battalion, France

                August 4, 1917

Dear Mother,

 Recv'd your letter of July 9th and no need to tell you I was pleased to hear from you. I was down to the base the other day on business and was talking to Major Jones, Bervil Watling*, and Bon Gormely. The major has a "bomb proof" job there for the duration. Colonel Mersereau is also there, but I did not have time to look him up. But I did not lose any sleep over it. As I think only for him the 132 Battalion may have got over here as a unit…

 I suppose the clergy is doing a rushing business with the slackers. They will all be getting married now to dodge conscription…Well I must close now for the mail will go in an hour and I have to write my London *Jane*. Well goodbye for now, love to all,

 Frank

---

* Bervil W. Watling (2001353) born at Chatham, NB, July 1894, joined at Newcastle December 1916.

PART THREE
France & Belguim

FINALLY TO THE CONTINENT

To finally arrive on the continent was what these men had been waiting for. They had joined up to fight and getting to France or Belgium was a watershed event. Art Robinson was from Tryon, PEI, and had travelled to Saint John in the autumn of 1914 to join the "Fighting 26th." He tells his aunt of random shell fire, maimed troops and the international composition of his battalion. Although Willie Muir had joined the 115th New Brunswick Infantry Battalion, through no fault of his own, he ended up in the 127 Battalion (York Rangers of Ontario). This unit in turn was converted into the Second Battalion, Canadian Railroad Troops. Willie tells his mother of hearing the big guns, of living in huts, of tearing up track, and of seeing German prisoners—all reputedly well out of the danger zone! Finally, Horace Morell, who married one month before joining up, relates to his mother how he, the last to join, beat his brothers Fred and Herb to France and the front. He regrets not having heard from his new wife, Hazel, since he left Woodstock. In an effort to be helpful, he suggests to his mother that Hazel should spend some time the coming winter with his mother in Newcastle instead of living and worrying alone in Spring Hill, just outside of Fredericton.

Arthur Robinson
2nd Canadian, E Force
26th Battalion, 5th Brigade, France

August 30, 1915

Dear Aunt Robbie,

I received your very welcome letter last night. I was very glad to hear from you. How did you find the old home this time? I suppose everything will be changed quite a bit since you was home last. Of course, we all know that such change must take place sooner or later and that it is useless to mourn our loss to too great an extent. God's will is the law and He knows best. I am seeing sights every day that will make a person but believe the firmer in the Almighty Power who is guiding.

When a person sees two chums walking across the camp ground together and one is struck dead with lightning [a shell] while the other is left standing with little more than a shock, it certainly makes one think. Again, when you see the hundreds of maimed soldiers, some far worse off than if they were dead and when nearly daily train loads of freshly wounded men pass right under your eyes, it makes you wonder at the ups and downs of this human life.

Just a few days ago I saw a Red Cross train going one way with wounded while a big troop train was going the other way with hundreds of boys and men off for the front to take the place of the ones who had fallen. It sounds queer but it is true that we are all anxious to see this thing through. Every day some new troops go but the rest "kick" because it wasn't their battalion. It is whispered about that this "outfit" of ours is going to relieve the Canadians who are at the front before long. We are all wishing it is true.

The First Canadian Division did some of the most distinguished work ever accomplished on the battlefield and the 2nd Division are determined that they will keep up the good name won for us through some of the best blood of dear old Canada.

You should just see the bunch of men there is in the 26th alone. They are a magnificent body of fellows all right, and this platoon I am in is a corker and there are, I don't know how many different nationalities in it—Indian, French, Russians, Belgians, English, Irish, Scotch, Americans, and Canadians. Some mob, eh? You can hear nearly any language around here any time of day.

Believe me they are a vicious-sounding bunch when some of their old friends drop in to see them, with his head bandaged up, or on a pair of crutches, or without an arm, or something wrong which can be charged up to the Huns.

If the Germans get all that these 26th fellows say they will, it is time for them to quit.

Say there is a fellow right here at the table with me and he just asked me who I was writing to and when I told him, he said to tell you he will go up to see you with me as soon as the war is over, if you promise you will have a couple of nice girls there for us and lots of "dough"— for we will be a bit hard up if money is as scarce as it is now.

I will have to close with the promise too—I will write you again before we leave England. So I will say goodbye. With lots of love from your nephew,

Arthur Robinson

William A. Muir
127th Battalion
Canadian Railway Troops

January 28, 1916

Dear Mother,

Somewhere in France enjoying life as much as possible in wartime. We ain't in the trenches nor won't be, I guess. We have been moving for nearly three weeks now, but where we're at for now you can hear the big guns nice and plain. And they sound good to me when we are far away from them. We are working building huts and taking up track and sending it to the front. There ain't no danger where we are now. We have great fun buying things in France; wee, wee and French is all they will say... There ain't no news and I can't say what I want to anyway. There is a lot of German prisoners here where

we are. I have made a lot of mistakes in this letter but I am in bed or nearly in bed anyhow. We don't have much time to write now so I ain't going to write very often so I will say goodbye, from
   Willie

Horace Morell
8th Field Army Brigade CFA, *France*

November 16, 1916

Dear Mother,

I have been a long time making up my mind to write. I haven't had much chance as I've been pretty busy. It is getting pretty blamed cold here now. We had a heavy frost here this morning. It makes a fellow begin to look for a pair of the old woolen hand sox.

There is three or four of us sleeping in a shack made of canvas bags with a steel roof on it, and believe me we get all the nice cool air that is going. We never take our clothes off at all. For all that I am quite contented here and am running away with the idea that I'll be on my way to Canada this time next year.

It seems strange that I was the last of the three to enlist and got to the land of the big noise first.* I don't suppose Fred or Herb will be over here before January or February as they will have three or four months training in England. Fred didn't like to see me coming so soon, but I wasn't fussy as I didn't like England a little bit.

I wonder how Hazel* is getting along. I haven't got a letter from her since I left Woodstock. In fact, I haven't heard from anybody,

---

* Horace's two brothers, Fred and Herb, had also joined the CEF.
* Hazel Gallop, Horace's wife, of Springhill, NB, whom he married one month before joining the battery.

but I ought to be getting some mail soon now. It will sure be good when it does come.

I wish Hazel would go over and stay a month or so with you this winter if you are alone. It would break the monotony of Springhill.

I really don't know what address to give you as I am only attached to this unit I am with now and liable to move any day to something else. I will wait for a day or two and see what turns up.

Will you send me Jennie's [sister] address so that I can drop her a line now and then. I suppose she is in Montreal by this time.

W. Horace Morell.

I will send you some souvenir as soon as I get a hold of something worthwhile. Tell Jim I'll bring him a German helmet. Must close now, but will write again in a few days.

Sincerely yours,
W. H. M.

P.S.: Send me a "Leader" now and again so that I can get some of the war news. We hear nothing here. WHM

FIRST TIME TO THE TRENCHES

Baptism of fire was literally true for these men. Both Lockhart and Lawlor relate the excitement of their first tour of the trenches. Lawlor uses the two most common terms for the enemy—the Hun and Fritzie. They relate their experience of incessant rifle fire and the much more impersonal and deadly artillery bombardments. Lockhart is impressed by the attitude and spirit of the men under his command—even the wounded. Both relate close calls and despite the bravado, Lawlor revealingly ends by telling his sister Clare to instruct their younger brother Joe to "stay in Canada."

Lieutenant Frank Lockhart
26th Battalion, Belgium

October 4, 1915

Just have time for a short note so will write on these postcards which I bought in a little town near our billets. They are on sale at all the little towns in France. They give you a great idea of the power of the modern high explosive shells. Have had a week in the first line trenches and can tell you I enjoyed it immensely! At times rifle fire was brisk and we were shelled several times, but it was more fun than anything else. At the last of it the field guns were a welcome change from the incessant rifle fire; got showered several times but with one exception which I will tell you about later. One high explosive shell hit my parapet in one place (my platoon had considerably over two hundred yards to defend) and blew the whole thing into the trench and completely buried two men. I had just passed a minute or two before. The men all thought it great—a great joke and laughed uproariously. It took over a hundred sandbags to fill the hole. Fortunately, I had intended improving the trench that night, so had filled 158 that afternoon so had them all ready. So you see in this business a little preparedness goes a long way.

Bill T* was the first of the battalion to get wounded. It did not hurt him at the time but was painful afterwards. He proved to be full of grit. They started to carry him on a stretcher, but they got tired, (the trench was so narrow and crooked), so Parker Gallant carried him on his back. P. did himself out so they sent him away for a rest. He is a great boy and luckily as strong as a horse. He told me Bill never gave in but put one arm around his neck and hung on like a good fellow. The men are a perpetual wonder to me. They swing right into the work like veterans and they sure have nerve. I am proud to have command of such a party.

Several days were nothing but rain so we were wet to the skin and covered with mud, but there wasn't a whimper out of anybody. They sure are a peach of a bunch. All our Petitcodiac boys are well and in good spirits. Saw Bremner last night. He is fine and a corporeal now, also saw Henry Gogan—he looks as hard and as tough as nails. So does Walter Arthur.⁺

Am not allowed to tell you where we are or what units are next to us but are sure in a pretty place. Have seen a lot of boys of the first division and they say this is one of the prettiest countries they ever saw. I can well believe it. It is a great country for trees along the roads. Every little way there are avenues flanked with enormous elms, about forty or fifty feet high, trimmed at the bottom but meeting at the top. Lovely and shady on a hot day.

Think I told you all about going up to Sodens and how nice they were to me. They had a beautiful garden and one pear tree in particular was a regular pet. It contained the largest pears I ever saw, also the largest number. It was literally loaded down. Well, yesterday I got a lovely box from them. It contained three jars of lovely homemade...
[the text ends here]

- William D. Turnbull (69986) born in Stanley, NB, and his next of kin was his mother, Bessie, who lived in Petitcodiac, NB.

⁺ The men mentioned are Allan Hugh Bremner (69043) who joined the 26th Battalion at Saint John on November 5, 1914; Henry Gogan (69337) of Petitcodiac who joined the 26th Battalion at Saint John on November 13, 1914; and Walter H. Arthur (69022) of Petitcodiac, who joined the 26th Battalion at Saint John on November 28, 1914.

Lieutenant Frank Lawlor
87th Battalion, France

May 23, 1917

Dear Clare,

Suppose you will be kind of worried for not hearing from me sooner. But have been pretty busy the last eight to ten days. We have been very close to Fritzie. My first experience and it sure was a good one, but I stood it up til the last night. Unfortunately, I sprained myself and the result is I am in hospital this three days, but will be out and with the battalion by the time you get this note. Still address any mail to 87th—it will always get me for they know where I am at all times.

The fourth morning I came off duty in the front line. I went to my dugout with Fred Mowat* and to my surprise I received the box with the cake, socks, and chocolates, and believe me they sure went good. Mowat and I certainly done justice to them. I really don't know how much to thank you. I sure did enjoy them and only hope I can pay you back some way.

We are having lovely weather over here now. It is fine when the sun shines in the trenches, but hell when it rains.

I got a good baptism the night I went in. The Hun must have put over ten thousand shells and everyone seemed to break about ten yards from you. But strange to say I did not mind it after a bit. But you tell Joe⁺ for me to be sensible and stay in Canada. As for myself, I like the life fine. There is always some adventure to it, always something doing. Well Clare, I must say goodbye now as news is scarce. Drop a

---

* Lieutenant Fred T. Mowat of Campbellton, NB, who was a brother officer with Frank in the 132 Battalion.
+ Frank's younger brother Joseph, born in 1895.

PART THREE : FRANCE & BELGUIM

line soon and thank you and mother once more for your box. Write soon, brother,

Frank

Excuse the paper and pencil—all we have here.

LIFE AT THE FRONT: THE INFANTRY

Rarely did the infantry write while in the trenches; it was too dark, too dirty, too dangerous, and they were too on edge and too tired. Letters were received and written when at the rear at rest or when in the hospital system recovering from minor wounds. Frank Lawlor writes to his mother while recovering from such an injury. He relates his first trip to the trenches as a junior officer. Although they were in a support role, waiting to go to the actual front trench, a task was handed him—erecting barbed wire, at night, in the dark, while the enemy shelled the area they were working in. The experienced scout leading them to the site remarked that the shelling was bad and that Frank would have to make the call—he decided to proceed. He was lucky. He and all his men escaped unharmed despite the constant shelling. Frank commented on the smell. It was summer and the unburied dead of both sides lay everywhere.

Eight months later in the winter of 1918, William Hape of the 85th Nova Scotia Battalion wrote his father. He wrote from a dugout. By this stage of the war each side possessed so much heavy artillery that the trenches had ceased to exist. Soldiers either stayed in shell holes or far underground in dugouts twenty to thirty feet deep. Hape had seen much combat. He tells his dad of many near misses, of having his puttee cut by a bullet and of losing his close friend R. D. Hall. His war weariness is clear. He wishes he were home again. The long, drug out ending to his brief letter speaks volumes as to his heart's longing. Sadly, he, like Frank Lawlor, did not return home.

Lieutenant Frank Lawlor
87th Battalion, France

June 18, 1917

Dear Mother,

Just to let you know I am still on light duty, but am OK now and will soon join the 87th again. So you can always use for the address: 87th Canadians, France, and it will always get me quicker than any other as they always know where to find me.

We have been having beautiful weather lately. In fact, for the last month nothing but sunshine and a few showers to cool it off. I often hear from the boys in England and as yet there has been none of them sent over. We could have still been there if we wanted to, but I am glad I came over for I am used to it now and don't mind it. The first time is always the worst. I tell you the first night will make your hair curl under shell fire. There is no one can tell me he is not a little nervous the first time.

Did I tell you about my first night? Well, if I did it is no harm to tell you again. We were out in reserve at the time and were going in the front line next day. About 8:30 PM an order came in to the 87th for a working party and thirty men to report to the battalion on our left. Being in A Company and No. 1 platoon I had to take it. I reported to where the order called for, and I thought to myself this is a good job away behind the lines; but when I got my orders I found I had to wire and dig a trench in front of a position that had been taken two hours before by our troops. And the Huns were bent on getting it back.

Well I met the scouts and they informed me that in the front line the shelling was awful and to use my own judgement if I would undertake the job. The way I looked at it was if I go back and say it was too heavy, the fire, what would the O. C.* think of me and my first trip? So I told the scouts to lead on. On we went and up the valley and the shells light everywhere around us. The corporal who was with me says you sure are getting it for the first time. He had been over here 18 months and said the shelling was worse than he had seen for some time. Well to make a long story short, we done the job and came out without a casualty.

The next day we took the front line for ____⁺ days. The first day in, I came off of duty at 4:00 AM and was just turning in for my four hours sleep and the adjutant came in. He asked me if I was in charge of the working party at Foss 6. I said "Yes Sir" and said here is where I get it for something I've done wrong. So he handed me a letter and to my surprise, it was from the O. C. of the battalion. He was writing and congratulating me on the fine work me and my party done under such heavy shell fire and then my own O. C. wrote me a very nice letter.

But I will tell you what: there were times when I would sooner have been in Newcastle than the valley when the shells were bursting not ten yards from us and did not know what moment one was going to land in the party and blow us all up.

The smell of the dead was that bad. The fellows said it was like dead man's valley on the Somme.

Well I must say goodbye for now,
Love to all, son,
Frank

---

* Officer Commanding.
⁺ At this point Frank scratched the number off the original letter.

William Kenneth Hape
85th Battalion, France

February 28, 1918

Dear Father,

Just a few lines to let you know that I am well. Hoping that this will find you all well at home. I am in a dugout. I couldn't go to sleep so I will try and drop you a few lines. Well there is nothing new out here—everything going on about the same old way. We've been having pretty warm weather, trenches have been pretty good. It is raining a little tonight, but I don't think it will amount to much.

Well, I suppose you are thinking about fishing again by this time. Well I suppose it is pretty dull around home now. How is Millidge now? I suppose he is still at home. I have been lucky since I struck France. There has been fellows wounded right alongside of me and I never got a scratch. I had a bullet to cut my puttie in two but never brought blood—if I had've got it in the leg I would have been in Blighty. But this time I lost one of my best chums, who has been together here since we have enlisted. He was from Port Dufferin—R. D. Hall.* There ain't many of us together now. They are leaving one by one, but I have an idea that I am going to see old Canada again. I haven't saw any of the boys from home for some time. I would like to be at the old shop this summer. I hope you have good luck and do well.

I haven't heard from home for some time. I have sent you a photo that I had taken in Blighty while on leave. Let me know if you received it safe or not. I would write to all, but there is no news that I can say so one letter will do for all. I think I have done pretty good for this time. I am going to try and have a sleep so I will close. From your loving son Kenneth, somewhere in France to dear Father and mother and all the

---

* Robert Douglas Hall (223538) born in Sheet Harbour, NS, 1891. Joined in Halifax April 1916.

PART THREE : FRANCE & BELGUIM

rest at home wishing you all best wishes. You spoke about G. Baker being killed. Was it G. Baker in Wallace or was he out here?

So goodbye, hoping to hear from you soon again, good night to all!

LIFE AT THE FRONT: THE ARTILLERY

As the war lurched onwards, both sides attempted to break the trench stalemate by increasing the amount and size of artillery fired. Before battles, the goal was to utterly destroy the opposing sides' barbed wire and trench systems. At all times, the goal was to destroy and harass the enemy and render movement for kilometres behind his lines highly dangerous to impossible. The number of shells fired climbed into the millions. By 1917, barrages would include high explosive, shrapnel, and a mixture of gases. Under these circumstances, the opposing artillery became a necessary target. Willie Muir tells his mom something he saw happen to a gun crew one day. William Drake describes his first trip "up to the lines"—the artillery firing line at the front. His battery was subjected to a counter-battery barrage which he describes in great detail. Chisholm MacDonald, writing from hospital, relates his hatred of gas, the dangers of sound ranging, and a most interesting tale of his heavy gun battery's first action—destroying a house kilometres distant which was used as a German telephone exchange. Fred Morell fills out the picture as he tells his mother how his battery caught a German infantry counter attack out in the open and annihilated them. The realities of modern, mechanized warfare were altering these men and their world and they were sharing this transformation with mothers and sisters back home.

William A. Muir
Horton War Hospital
Epson, Surrey, England

October 27, 1917

Dear Mother,

*J*ust a line to let you know that I am well and having a good time in this country—better than France…Well there ain't much news to write so I will not write much, but will tell you one thing that I saw happen. There was a gun crew of about five or six men around the gun—they were not in action but was sitting around the gun pit and a shell dropped in there. And one was wounded terrible bad and one other was wounded not very bad and one not hurt at all and the others were picked up on stretchers in pieces about as big as your hat and a lot smaller and none any bigger and that is only one thing I saw. That is a common thing, but I won't say any more about it, but things like that don't bother a man at all out there. He would mind it some back there home. When you go digging you dig up bones and so forth… *(remainder of letter missing)*

Arthur William Drake
62nd Battery, France

September 27, 1917

Dear Charlotte,

J suppose you will think I am dead or very near for not writing before, but I have been kept going ever since we came over here. We are having fine weather, no rain and not hot, but I expect the bad times will soon be here for rain and mud.

I have been up the lines on the guns for the past three weeks and seen some pretty exciting times and plenty of hard work which seems to be the main thing around our battery. We had very little trouble from being shelled until three days ago when I think they got wise to where we were and started shelling us with heavy artillery all one day and made us get to our dugouts for the day. He dropped one shell on the side of our gunpit and set fire to it, so six of us ran down to put it out which was a very foolish thing to do as he could see us and poured in shells—about four a minute so we had to run for cover. And anybody that was watching us seen a funny sight as we were diving into old shell holes with empty cases in the bottom every time a shell came over as you think they are going to land on the back of your neck, they were so close. I hadn't time to pick out the soft spots like Susie and I did when we heard the boat whistle while we were in the back field. We got off lucky as nobody got hurt, but the gun I was looking after was broken up and put out of action and I was sent back with it to the shops for repairs, so will have a few nights rest which I certainly need for while up at the guns you are either working or the Germans are putting over gas to worry you with.

Well you will think this is a pretty gloomy letter, but I have enjoyed the experience so far and with a little luck I think I will be alright, but if anything should happen to me Father will hear first and will you then send Hattie* word by wire collect? Also, if you have a pair of mittens to spare, will you send them along for the winter as I can't buy anything like that over here. Well I must close for this time, hoping you are all well. I am feeling fine,

Yours truly,
Arthur (write often)

---

* Alfred's sister.

Chisholm D. MacDonald
No. 5 Siege Battery
Canadian Convalescent Hospital

October 30, 1917

Dear Margaret,

I met two others from the battery here in this hospital. One was wounded early in the summer and is going back to Canada next Friday, as the tendon at the back of his ankle was cut and he will be always lame. The other fellow was gassed and he expects to go to Canada too as his heart was affected by the gas.

I tell you that gas is one thing I don't like as it is as apt to affect a person afterwards. The night before I went to the hospital, when I was lying sick in the billets, the Huns sent over gas, and I had to put on my mask, sick as I was.

The artillery are getting an awful lot of casualties from the new German gas shells now. Whenever they cannot get a direct hit on the guns, they send over a barrage of gas shells all around, which burst whenever they touch anything and fill the air with the gas. The infantry do not get it so bad for they are so handy to the Germans that the enemy gets as much as they do if he puts any over on them.

Artillery used to be a lot safer than infantry but there is not much difference between them now, for you cannot conceal a battery as formerly on account of the "sound ranging" instruments, built on the plan of a seismograph, which detects the exact spot of a hostile battery that is firing, so that in a few minutes you know where to land your shells to put that battery out of action.

We all thought it very exciting work when we went to the front first. I remember the first time we fired. The intelligence department had found out that a certain house which was miles behind the lines, and which was half broken down, was in reality a large telephone exchange which should at once be destroyed. We were the only battery around which could reach it, and we got orders to put it out of business at once. This was on April 12th, three days after Vimy Ridge was taken, and just as we had finished two days labour getting the gun in position. Everybody was excited and nervous and all the hands off duty crowded around, standing on tiptoe with their hands to their eyes waiting for the explosion. The major was doing the observing out at an O.P.* and his orders came over the phone, "Fire!" and the four guns one after the other sent their two-hundred-pound shells toward the target. There was nothing heard for about half a minute, during which time the guns were reloaded, and then "All guns 30° more right." Everybody heaved a sigh of disappointment, for the first shell had evidently gone to the left of the target, but once more came the "Fire" and the gun jumped backward with the shock of the explosion. Another pause, and then another correction came over the phone, and the elevation of the guns was changed slightly. This time you could hear the strained silence before the guns spoke again, and sent their freight on its deadly errand. Almost before the echo of the shots had died away, there came the exultant news that we now had the right range and two of our shells had got direct hits on the house, which was now a heap of ruins. There was one more order, "Empty guns," and the guns which had been reloaded were fired, at the same elevation, sending their shells into what was left of the target. Then the gun barrel was cleaned out and the covering of chicken wire and boughs pulled over it to conceal its outline from the prying eyes of aeroplanes, and we all went to wash the mud off our hands before we got our supper, feeling that our long period of training was over, and that we were now soldiers indeed, a part of the "Empire's fighting line," and perhaps thinking rather regretfully of the human beings who had been living but a few minutes before, and whom we had blown out of the world.

---

* Observation Post.

Last time I wrote, I gave you my address, but in case that letter should have gone astray, here it is again: Canadian Convalescent Hospital, Bearwood Park, Wokingham, Berks.

So long for now,
Chisholm

Herbert Morell
CFA *Battery, France*

November 15, 1917

Dear Mother,

I'm not very busy today so I might as well write a few lines. There is really nothing to write about, but I know you are always glad to get a letter even if it is only a short one.

Well, we certainly put one over on Fritz a few nights ago. Just about dawn he made a desperate attempt to take back some of the ground he lost during the past few weeks. Our artillery put up a barrage that caught him just about right. The scrap didn't last more than an hour, but by the that time there were enough dead Fritzies in no man's land to make a year's supply of butter for the Fatherland...

I may have to go up to the guns again this afternoon although I just came down yesterday. There is very little sleep for us up there, and it's a warm place so we change gun crews every second day. Fred is up there now. He is a cool one when we are on the receiving end of a straff, and nothing seems to bother him...

Must close now and write to Jennie*.

Love to all, from
Herb
#793942
Gunner A. H. Morell

---

* Herbert's wife.

PART THREE : FRANCE & BELGUIM

CHRISTMAS IN THE TRENCHES

Lieutenant Frank Lockhart
26th Battalion, Belgium

December 25, 1915

Dearest Mother,

Well here it is Christmas night and I am alone in my dugout. A dandy large dugout, large enough for three like me but as I am fortunate enough to be a platoon commander, I am entitled to a dugout all to myself. I am lying on my bed on my tummy writing this by the light of a candle. Can't you picture me? My dugout is not high enough to stand up in but can sit up nicely so haven't much to kick about have I? Do you realize this is the first xmas I ever spent away from home? I can tell you I realize it. Suppose you were all thinking about me today. Well, all day I was so busy I hadn't much time to think, but tonight I am thinking and wondering what you are all doing. Hope you are all well. I am. I can assure you, and with the exception of a slight cold, I never felt better in my life.

Will describe yesterday and today to you. These two days were much like any other and not at all like Christmas. Yesterday it rained hard and flooded out our kitchen, so today I put the men to building another on higher ground. Over here there is practically never any snow but lots of rain, so we have to do the best we can. The wind is awful. The land here is very rich and you can dig yards into the ground anywhere around and never find a stone so you can imagine how muddy it sometimes gets. When I tell you I never saw mud in Canada to equal it you can have a little idea what it is like. Got up this morning at eight and had breakfast consisting of lovely breakfast bacon, bread, butter, jam, and tea. Not too bad is it?

Loafed around, then Harry Ferguson gave me a large piece of xmas cake he got from home. (Your parcel did not arrive yet.) This filled me up so I could not eat any dinner. Right after dinner we got busy and started our kitchen. Had about twenty men filling sandbags. Twenty carrying brick and the rest carrying sandbags and piling them. We built a kitchen about 15 x 10 feet and have it nearly done. One of my men is a good bricklayer and he is making a big fireplace for us. I can crawl into the fireplace so you know it isn't small. A lot larger than the one at home. It is interesting doing this, but imagine this as a way of spending xmas. Not a speck of frost in the ground.

This afternoon some of the Germans got bold and thought as it was Christmas they would visit us, etc. A few rounds of shrapnel soon put them under cover again. Personally, I want nothing to do with them, and as for arranging a temporary Armistice, they can count me out. They are not to be trusted, and I don't give them any chance words. I do not allow any of my men to take unnecessary risks. My platoon has been singularly lucky, by long odds, the luckiest in the battalion. Had my first man wounded last trip in. He is all so far. The platoon next least has lost about eight so you see I am lucky. There are

Frank Lockhart digging practice trenches in England.

PART THREE : FRANCE & BELGUIM

sixteen platoons—over two hundred casualties, so you can figure out the average for yourself.

For supper tonight we had canned tomatoes, Heinz salad beans, with Bully Beef and walnut sauce, plum pudding, and tea. How is that for a feast? I couldn't have eaten another bit no matter how tasty it might have been. The plum pudding was sent to every man in the British army by the people. That is, an amount was collected and the pudding bought and sent to us. Very kind and thoughtful wasn't it? Tonight is very quiet. The Germans never fired a big gun all day. Will get a good sleep as I am in the front line tonight but am in support. A great difference I can tell you though after all the front line is really the best place to be in. Well dear mother, I got parcels from Mr. and Mrs. Humphreys, Grace Wilmot, Ina, and friends in England. It was mighty kind and thoughtful of them. I can tell you, I appreciate it and hope to be able to return the good deed sometime. Oh yes, got xmas cards from friends in Joggins, candy from a friend in Oxford, and cake and candy from Mary Mandry in Dorchester. They sure are all trumps.

Well mother dear this isn't much of a letter, but I hope it will be worth the time we both spend on it. Wishing you all a very Happy New Year which means all the boys home again and love and kisses to all,

Lovingly,
Frank*

---

* Written on a series of postcards; Petitcodiac War Museum reference number: 2006.3.68.s, z and y, rr, ss, tt.

PART FOUR

The Reality of War

ON THE LOSS OF A FRIEND

Sudden, random, unpredictable death was a constant reality of life at the front and for kilometres behind the lines. The following letters provide a powerful and moving witness to this reality. Both George Chapman and Willie Muir relate the death of close friends—termed "chums" in the vernacular of the times. Both were killed by artillery fire. The death of Willie's friend clearly had a profound effect on him for after he learnt of Dow's death he greatly reduced his volume of letter writing. Similarly affected, Fred Morell had the gut-wrenching task of writing his mother after the death of his brother Horace, who served in the same artillery unit.

The last two letters are unique. They concern the death of Waldo William Anderson of McKees Mills, NB, during the great Canadian advance of August 1918. One letter is from his company's commanding officer, Lieutenant Ganong, who was also in the battle and knew Waldo formerly when they were both in the 104th Battalion. The other letter is from Waldo's chum, Arnold Wright, who was very close to Waldo when he was hit. Arnold removed Waldo's 5th Canadian Mounted Rifles cap and collar badges from his body in order to send them to his relatives—his family still has them.

George T. Chapman
185th Battalion CEF, Somewhere in France

April 24, 1917

Dear Mary,

*G*ot ahead of you again. Got one of your letters here dated 13th March also one 18th and nothing else to do but answer the two in one. Now will you believe this—I can trim you every time.

Do you notice anything strange? Getting quite showy. Real writing paper and ink instead of a few leaves out of an old notebook and bad pencil and not only that, but written with a real Cape Breton pen. That one with the nice gold ban on it and the nice writing on it. Some class for this chicken—wait 'til I tell you; also sitting writing in a real room, of a real house, at a real table. Now you will be wondering how all this had happened.

Well, the battalion which I have been with since coming to France has orders to disband, and I am one of the boys who are to do the winding up of the records so therefore the comfortable quarters just mentioned. Last Thursday night, the 19th—I would mark on a calendar if I had one—do you know what happened? I slept on one of those household articles I have only had faint visions of since Alex and I were on that memorable pleasure trip last November. A BED. Didn't it feel good? You bet your life it did.

You will likely get a new address shortly for after this work is through I will transfer to some other battalion—likely to the 85th.

Now I have to write you the part of this letter that I would much rather have circumstances such that it would be unnecessary. What I would like to write is that our friend Murray* is OK and wished to be remembered to you, but as you are aware by this time, Murray has passed over the "great divide." He met the death of a soldier and a man. On the night of the 10th he was at his post in one of the trenches when a shell hit and severely wounded him. He was taken to hospital. I did not see him at the time of his wounding as my duties were in another part of the line and did not hear of it for two days later. I then looked up the stretcher-bearer who had dressed him and he gave me encouraging news telling me that altho' the wounds were severe they appeared to be only surface. However, the news came in on the 17th that poor Murray had passed away in hospital. I intend writing his people tonight. Believe me I miss my old buddy.

Say I got that box of fudge all right, also discovered some "huch" underneath, stowed away. Wonder who sent that? It was all dandy.

---

* Murray J. McInnis (878222) born 1891 at North Sydney, joined 185 Battalion in April 1916.

Am now on the lookout for those snaps. Won't I be pleased to see some of the old familiar faces. Will scan them very closely to see if I can detect any changes.

How is Maddie? Have not heard from her for some time. Bet then she is busy. Sure she is. Next letter you write, Mary, get Alex's correct address. My letters don't seem to get him with the address I have at present and no doubt Alex's thinking I am not answering him. He has not written me for some time.

I hear there is a Canadian mail in tonight, so if there is a letter of yours in it, you will have a speedy answer, as times are of the best for correspondence.

Remember me to all my old friends. Hope this finds you in your usual good health. With kindest regards and best wishes,

I am, as ever, your pal,

George

William A. Muir
Horton War Hospital,
Epson, Surrey, England

November 4, 1917

Dear Mother,

Just a line to let you know that I am well and having a good time here and got about a half a dozen letters from you and a lot this morning. I was glad to hear from you again. I was three weeks without any mail on account of moving around, but it will come better now since it is started. The next time you send a box don't put any soap in for it spoils everything else. It even made the chocolates taste but did not hurt the peppermints nor maple sugar, but the cake was awful all together—just like eating soap.

Well you asked me about Dow.* I know as much about him as you do but where he is missing so long they must know that he is not a prisoner. And I tell you when you get blew all to pieces as big as a hat it is impossible to tell who he was or what he did belong to and they can put it down that they will never see him in this world again. It is hard to say, but it is all for the best. But if I could only explain what it is like I have been nearly buried myself more than once. All covered, you have to crawl out of the mud the best way you can. But I am out of it now for a while but Mrs. Roberts⁺ need not look for Dow to write for I know pretty near what has happened to him for I have seen things like that happen before too much.

Well that is one question answered—I will start on the other one. We work from different places. We work from some little place where there is a railway centre and lay light steel up to the line. And sometimes we are up so close that old Willie* [Germans] uses his machine gun on us, but we generally do that at night. And when you hear the machine gun bullets whizzing around your ears you will dive for a hole and stay there 'til it is done, then crawl out. We have been at Ypres ever since we went to Belgium and when the push started we followed it up with the track, and they was going on when I left but I ain't had any word from there since I came over here. I can't write it down but hope to get back and will tell you then Mother, it is *awful, awful, awful*—ain't a name for it.

Our camp was handy a little village when we first came up to Belgium, but when the grand push started we had to hike it up the line farther.

You asked me if we worked on Sunday. Well we certainly did and I had about three or four Sundays off all the time I was over there, but we had two weeks rest last month. I guess it was last month. We had

---

* George Dow Roberts (742641), a close friend of Willie's also from Clarendon Station, NB. Dow transferred to the 26th NB Infantry Battalion and was killed on August 15, 1917. As he has no known grave, his name appears on the Vimy Memorial. He was twenty-two years old at the time of his death.

⁺ Dow's mother.

* Germans.

PART FOUR : THE REALITY OF WAR

two hours drill in the morning and the day to do as we liked, and there was a little town right handy and lots of hop fields and we used to help them pick hops. And one thing and another like that.

You spoke of not sending anything of Dow's home. Well he would have his small kit with him such as razor and brushes and things like that and the rest would be back at the battalion headquarters. And when he was reported missing they would take his things and give them to someone else and what he had with him would be broke if he was all blowed to pieces and if they was not hurt someone else would pick them up pretty quick. Now as I have explained the best I could on paper you will be able to form an idea about what would become of his stuff and why none of it was sent home. So I will close for now; with love to all, bye, bye,

Willie Muir—Write soon

Fred Morell
Somewhere in France

August 14, 1918

Dear Mother,

I have never before felt less like writing a letter than I do at present, but will try to get one off to you this morning while I have a few quiet moments. Nothing has ever upset me as Horace's[*] death has, and try as I may to stop thinking about it, I find it impossible to do. I always stayed in his shack or bivouac or whatever it happened to be when at the wagon lines, and naturally we always had our belongings more or less mixed, and a dozen times a day I come across some little

---

[*] Horace was Fred's brother. Fred and his other brother, Herb, served in the Canadian artillery and both survived.

thing or other that brings back to my mind some incident, time, and place, etc, when he was with us. I do not feel so badly as regards myself, but I worry continually about you and Hazel[*] and the rest at home. I realize fully what a terrible blow it must be to you all, but it is a great consolation for us all, to know that he died an honourable death, and for a cause that the world knows is right. We can feel almost proud that he died when he did when we think of the manner in which some people meet their death. There has never been a casualty in the battery that has caused deeper regret, for Horace was very popular indeed. The officers, especially the O.C. and the captain, have both spoken to Herb and me in very sympathetic terms and I think intend writing to you or father and also to Hazel. The captain has very kindly written to the officer commanding the hospital or field ambulance where he died, to get the location, name of the place, etc, where they buried him, and when this advance is over that we are engaged in at present, we can get a chance to see that the grave is fixed up and if I possibly can, I will have a good substantial cross put up and get a photo of it to send you.

Now I won't dwell on the subject any longer, Mother, for after all, there isn't much that I can say. I might tell you about the accident though, for I know you would like to know all about it. I was at the wagon lines that night, as the opposite relief to mine was at the guns, but I went up the next morning and saw the place and found out all I could from the boys who were there. He went up the night before to do some work in preparation for this great Canadian advance which started the next morning. He was hit about midnight and was carried immediately to the nearest dressing station, so you can rest assured that he received all the attention and care that human hands could give him. He was hit in the back and the left lung was punctured. The boys who carried him to the dressing station say that he regained consciousness on the way down and spoke to them as though there was nothing the matter. One fellow said that he had as much pluck and

---

- Horace's wife, now widowed, lived in Springhill, NB.

grit as two ordinary men. I wish I could have got to the hospital to see him before he died, but it was impossible as I knew nothing of it until the next morning and by then I was in the strafe myself and we were advancing by the mile. I might say that we are still going, so the place where our guns were then is miles to the rear of us, so there is a certain consolation in knowing that the German shells will never disturb his grave.

I must close for this time, but will write as often and as soon again as I can. I would like to write Hazel again, if I wasn't so awfully busy but you might send her this if you wish. Poor Hazel, I feel sorrier for her than I can say, and I hope she does not take it too hard. Best regards to all the folks, and don't worry too much. Tell Jim that I have a German officer's cap to send him when I get a chance.

Your loving son,
Fred

Lieutenant H. N. Ganong*
5th Canadian Mounted Rifles (CMR), in the field

August 31, 1918

Mrs. W. Anderson,
McKees Mills, Kent Company, NB

Dear Mrs. Anderson,

*A*lthough you have no doubt been informed of the death of your son #709086 Private W. W. Anderson, I feel that you would derive some comfort from receiving a more personal communication than the necessary brief official notice.

---

* Lieutenant Hardy N. Ganong (3237) born in 1890 at St. Stephen, NB, formerly of the 104 Battalion (NB) and now a lieutenant in the 5 CMR and Waldo W. Anderson's commanding officer.

I have always felt a personal interest and pride in your boy since he came to this battalion as he was in my old platoon in the 104th Battalion in Canada. In France, as in Canada, he was always a splendid soldier and what was even greater, he always retained his high principles. Without doubt he was one of the cleanest living boys I have ever known and his crossing to the Great Beyond must be welcomed by those wonderful words, "Well done, good and faithful servant." I want you to know, Mrs. Anderson, that my appreciation of your son as a soldier was more than equalled by my admiration of him as a Christian gentleman. Quiet and unassuming, he nevertheless was known and loved by all the men of his company and his death is very keenly felt by all.

He was killed very early in the attack of August 26th and suffered no pain, his death being instantaneous. He is buried in a quiet little cemetery well behind the lines and his grave will always be kept sacred.

While his loss will naturally be a very hard blow to you, much of the sorrow of death will be relieved by the knowledge that he was prepared to meet his Maker, and that someday you will meet him in that Great Future where wars and heartaches shall be no more.

Memorial scroll from the King for the family of Waldo Wm. Anderson.

Please accept the most sincere sympathies of myself and the other officers and men of this company, and if there is the very slightest thing we can do please do not hesitate to let me know. Yours most sincerely,

H. N. Ganong, Lieutenant
5th C. M. R.
O. C., A Company

Arnold B. Wright
5 CMR, *France*

September 3, 1918

Dear Mrs. Anderson,

It is with deep regret that I write and tell you how sorry we all are that your son Waldo was killed. As I was his chum, and we were together most of the time since he came back to the battalion, I miss him perhaps more than some of the rest of the platoon. We have been in the same section and were advancing together when we saw some Huns with a machine gun a little on our right. And the section started over to mop it up. Waldo was a little ahead of the rest of us and as we got up quite close to the gun and was trying to see it in the mist he was hit in the head and was instantly killed. I went to him as soon as I could but he was unconscious. His face was calm and showed no sign of pain. It was as he wished it if it was to be the way. When we were talking the night before and wondering how we would get through, he said he would like to get a blighty and go back to Canada, but if he got it, he hoped it would be quick and painless.

I gave his pocketbook and letters to the clerk who said that they would be sent home. But his badges and watch chain that he got off a prisoner that he captured the 9th of April I am sending now. The scissors are a pair that he bought himself, either in Blighty or Canada before he came over here.

If there is anything that I could do, to oblige you, please write and let me know as I would be pleased to help you in any way I could. The whole platoon extend to the family their deepest sympathy for the loss of your son. I remain your sincere friend,
No. 710104
Private Arnold B. Wright, A Company*

CHANGES AND CHANCES

The unpredictable fortunes of war were not limited to battles, but also included matters of place and time. Specifically, life or death were often a matter of not being at certain places at certain times, in short, what might be called "luck." Frank Lockhart tells his dad how lucky his platoon had been up to that time—only three wounded. Sadly, Frank's personal luck ran out just three months later in April 1916. Willie Muir writes his mom from hospital telling her of an injury sustained during a wrestling session with his buddies. This was most fortuitous for a large draft of men from his unit were sent to France as infantry reinforcements while he was there. This draft included his best chum, Dow, who was killed a few months later. Finally, and saddest of all, is the story of Frank Lawlor. After serving in the trenches for some time he had applied and secured permission to train as a pilot. Frank was just about to get on the boat for England when all leave was cancelled in March of 1918. The cause was the massive German spring offensive which threatened to break the British lines. He hastily returned to the front and was killed just nine days after penning a hastily scribbled letter to his sister, Clare.

---

* Arnold B. Wright, born March 24, 1896, at Lower Southhampton, NB, joined 104 Battalion March 1916.

William Muir
Soldiers' Christian Assoc.

December 10, 1916

Dear Mother,

Just a line to let you know that I am well and having a good time and enjoying life as much as possible. We was on the range ten days. I was not down the last day, the day before the last, we had to parade one hundred yards with the gas helmets on and the next day we had to…two hundred…yards with them on. I went to the doctor and got light duty. I had a sore foot and he could not find any sores on it and I told him it was sore in the joint and he gave me light duty. We had to walk seven miles each way and the walking we had to do when we was there. We all have got colds. No matter where you go you can see fellows spitting up a lung…

Well you found out that I was in the hospital. I was not going to tell you at all, but when I went in I was going to tell you. Then I thought you would worry about me so I would keep still and not say anything about it, but we were fooling and tumbling around and I got a kick between the legs and hurt me. One of my testicles swelled up and that was what the matter was…Another fellow got his ribs cracked wrestling around and after I came out again another fellow got his leg broke the same way. So I ain't the only one. The reason I did not tell you before is that I did not like to speak about it so when anybody asks you what ailed me tell them I got hurt wrestling.

Well it is good that I did get hurt for if I had not I would've been in France. The most of the platoon went that I was in and if I had've been out of the hospital I would've went too. I sent you a box a while ago; did you get that yet? I ain't got any boxes yet at all, but am expecting them. It takes about six to ten weeks for them to come across. Well this is all, bye, bye, from

Willie—write soon—
Merry Christmas and Happy New Year

Lieutenant Frank Lockhart
26th Battalion, Belgium

Early January 1916

Dear Dad,

*J*ust have time for a short note. Sent one a few days ago which I hope arrived alright. I enclosed a handkerchief on which was some Belgium lace and am going to enclose another in this. Hope both arrive in good shape. What do you think of this card? If you can believe it, you can see the Canadians are some fighters. They are too! The box you expressed to me on November 18th reached me on January 3rd so you see it didn't come very fast, did it? That is a trick boxes have, but the fact that it arrived is the main thing. It sure was welcomed and contained just the right things. I intend writing Aunt Dell and Lottie tonight or tomorrow. It was mighty kind of them to send me so many nice things. I can't find that handkerchief now so will have to send it next time. The mails were so full xmas I did not send it then for fear it would get lost. The box of underwear and socks has not yet arrived but will likely be here in a few days. Boxes seem to take a long time, but we usually get them sometime.

Our weather is now lovely. The mornings are just like spring at home. Mild and pleasant and the birds singing hard enough to crack their throats. It is almost enough to make a fellow homesick if he had time enough to think about it which we haven't. Right now the grass is a bright green and the red roofs of the farmhouses make a contrast very pleasing to the eye. Suppose Will and Harry* have been home since you wrote. Would like to see them in khaki. I bet they were fine,

---

* Frank's two younger brothers. William (709679) was born 1893 and joined the 104 in November 1915. Harry (709579) was born in 1897 and joined the 104 in November 1915. Both went on to serve in the Fighting 26th. Another, younger brother, Robert (2303891) joined the Forestry Corp in May 1917.

smart-looking soldiers. Wish they would send me some snapshots. We sure have been lucky and my platoon the luckiest of all. So far I have had none killed and only three wounded. Two of these were done the last time in, so you see I have no luck coming. I hold the battalion record but am not bragging for we sure have had good luck. When it breaks I will have to look out. Your suppositions were perfectly correct. If we take part in any of the big drives we are sure to lose heavily. So far we practically have not been in action at all. The reports sure are not correct and that account of Carter's was a fright. He only had two trips to the trenches so hardly knew what he was talking about.

Glad Petitcodiac has done so well. For a village it has done wonderful work. If all do so well in proportion we will win this war in jig time. As it is now, it is just a matter of time. They have shot their bolt and now we will put them on the blink. They should have to pay for all the property they have destroyed also pay all the Allies for the money they expended. If this is done the world will never be troubled with German invasions again. I am arranging about that insurance policy. It is due in February but I have a month's grace so that makes due in March. I am arranging with Bank of Montreal now. Did Ina get home for xmas? Hope she did. Suppose the boys were there so after all you would have quite a house full. Hope Santa was good to you all and that you had a very merry Christmas and I hope 1916 will be the happiest and most prosperous of your life. Am enclosing a little note to Elsie.

Love to mother and yourself, sincerely,
*Frank**

---

* Petitcodiac War Museum; (PWM). 2006.3.68 x, r, q, p, o, n. the year is 1916.

Lieutenant Frank Lawlor

March 29, 1918

Dear Clare,

Just a line before reporting back to my unit. I am now at the Base. Had my transfer through, [and was] just going to get on the boat for England, when word came through that all leave and transfers were cancelled, <u>so you see I am out of luck</u>*, for I have to report back right away as we need all the officers and men we can get a hold of, especially those with some experience. I sure was disappointed, but it cannot be helped as we are here to win the war, if possible. Am in a great hurry to catch a train so will have to close—will write later,

Love to all,
Brother,
Frank

Frank Lawlor before going overseas.

---

* Frank had secured a transfer to the Royal Flying Corps, in effect escaping the trenches. He was killed nine days after he wrote this letter to his sister.

BATTLES

Canadians were involved in most of the major battles on the western front. The capture of Vimy Ridge was the first significant Allied victory of the war and was won by the Canadian Corp of 100,000 men fighting as a single unit for the first time. By First World War standards the victory was not especially costly at 3,600 Canadians killed. In the words of Herb Morell, in comparison with Passchendaele in November 1917, Vimy was a picnic. Relating conditions at Passchendaele, Herb speaks of deep mud as far as the eye could see, of wooden walkways, of constant shelling, and of being done for if one slipped off the zigzagging duck-boards.

With the withdrawal of Russia from the war in the autumn of 1917, the Germans were able to move all their troops from the eastern front and launch a massive spring offensive in March 1918. This last-ditch effort to win the war made significant advances, but Art Drake assures his sister that all they had won was kilometres of mud and at a horrific cost.

By August of 1918, it was the Allies' turn to strike at the exhausted and depleted German forces. The so-called Hundred Days Offensive, which ended the war, was spearheaded in part by the Canadians. Art Harrison of the Canadian Army Medical Corps (camc) relates his three weeks of hell caring for the Canadian wounded. There would be thousands more to come, for the Canadian forces sustained thirty percent of all their war casualties advancing victoriously during that final one hundred days. Finally, Charles McInnis writes his wife in late October confident that the war could not last much longer. The reason: the infantry were advancing so fast that the railroad building troops who repaired the lines the retreating Germans destroyed could not keep up with them. The end had to be near.

VIMY RIDGE

Lieutenant Frank Lawlor
13th Canadian Reserve Battalion
Shoreham by Sea, England

April 13, 1917

Dear Mother,

Just a line before going to dinner. I have been doing a little work lately as Captain Archer is gone on a course of instruction and I am in Command of B Company and I am getting a draft ready of two hundred men to reinforce the 26th Battalion in France and it sure is some job to get them equipped and ready to go.

I wrote Clare [sister] two days ago so I have told her all the news. We have some mess here but the food is so high it costs like the deuce—4 shillings last month per day.* That means $30 per month. Besides your clothes which is no small sum.

What do you think of the Canadians now after the French losing 135,000 men and trying to take Vimy Ridge for months. And the Canadians stepping in and taking the position in one day. The talk over here is the 26th Battalion made the final assault and held the ridge. I only wish I had have been into it...

I never enjoyed better health, never sick a day and always on the job. How is Kirt? Give him my best regards. Well mother dear, news around here is scarce so I must say goodbye for now. Best regards to Annie, Nell, and Clare.

Write soon,

son, Frank

---

* Officers ate in a different "mess" than the other ranks and enjoyed better food—but they had to pay for it. They also had to buy their own clothes.

PASSCHENDAELE

Gunner Herb Morell

December 5, 1917

Dear Mother,

It is not so frosty today so we feel a little bit better. Yesterday was an extra cold one. We had a "stand to" which lasted all night and we almost froze to death. When dawn came we found that the mud and water was frozen so solid that we could walk across country any place.

If you ever thought for a minute that you have seen mud and water you have made a mistake. Up at the guns and within a couple of miles of the guns, if a horse gets off of the plank road into the mud he's finished.

You may not know what part of the country we're in, but I can't tell you. Follow the movements of the Canucks and you won't be far astray. We keep together. As you already know we are in a flying brigade, attached to no particular division, but go when we are needed most. Our battery gets the name of being the crack battery of the brigade and since we struck this part, seven of our gunners have been decorated for their good work.

Our scrap last April was a picnic compared to this, but it is no use explaining as words can't express war of this kind. The human mind can't grasp it. All the training and lectures that I got on the effect of shells, etc., looks like ABC's now. At one time I thought I had a fair idea of war, after talking to men with experience, but I find France and the war too extensive to explain. Horrie might have told Hazel quite a lot, but you must figure that he is just as bomb proof as you are, and he never really was into a straff or mixed up in anything rough. The accuracy of the Boche's heavy guns is something that we all know too well, and as I once said before, I have a wholesome respect for his eight-and twelve-inch shells. Just to explain what I mean I'll give you an example of what he does.

The country is so broken up and turned over and over by shell fire that the troops have to build a trench mat track to walk on. It zigzags down from the front line to the roads several miles behind the guns. Fritz will start at the top of this walk and shell it all the way down. About every third or fourth shell will be a direct hit, the others will be a few yards to the left or to the right. The engineers fix it up and he blows it up again and so the war goes on. We are doing the same thing to him only we keep it up day and might and give him no rest. When it comes to guns we have them by the thousand and more ammunition than we can use in months.

We had a great time last September down at _____*. We took a couple of our guns (eighteen pounds) out into the open and used them for sniping. Winslow was observing for us and when he got his eye on anything we opened up. The fun of it was Fritz couldn't find us and he would sweep the place with his 4.1 shells but only once he came near us. It was certainly good fun.

I'm thankful that my nerves can stand the strain of this position we're in now. I feel sorrow for some of the men I see. Some are cold footed and haven't the sand in them to chase a yellow dog. But they don't belong to our army. Others can't control their nerves when a shell drops within a mile of them.

We have a Dane in our battery who certainly is a good man when it comes to a showdown. The other night he and I were on sentry duty at the guns. It was his first trip up as a gunner. Fritz let loose a few "black Marias"+ around us. I expected to see him get excited but he pulled a book of "Irish jokes" (yokes he called them) out of his pocket and started to read them to me. I sat on the seat of the gun and smoked a cigarette. When I got through and it was getting warm I said: let's beat it, Valleye. Walleye (we call him) says, "vell you was the old gunner, I

---

* Herb could not state the location for security purposes, so he left the space blank, essentially self-censoring.

+ A large German artillery shell that the troops could sometimes see coming at them.

vas vaiting for you to start." Any other new man would suggest it first thing.

Well I guess I've given you too much war news. I've been in France and Belgium longer than I expected to be and so far haven't told you a thing about the place. We read lots of letters in the papers written by some poor simps who never saw the war zone although they've been in France. But France is a big country. People in Canada don't know the difference, so they come to conclusions too easily. It's no cinch but I've never regretted the fact that I enlisted. I'm a volunteer and a great many can't say that. The Canadians will never be soldiers, they won't stand for it. They are just "fighting troops." We work together, fight with the Imps (Imperials) and Australians when the Fritizies are quiet. Our infantry won't keep quiet when in the line. They make trench raids and so forth. Taking it all through it's interesting, but I'd take my discharge any day. There is one thing about it though, we are well fed. It's marvelous when you see our rations being distributed all over the country to the different units. Nobody is left out...

Fred is a bombardier now and is up at the guns but will be down tomorrow. I'm due for going up in the morning. It's getting a little quieter now and it's about time.

I think I've written about enough for now so I'll close and answer one of the letters I got about a month ago. Best wishes for Christmas.

Love to all,

Herb

THE GERMAN SPRING OFFENSIVE OF 1918

Arthur W. Drake
France
              April 15, 1918

Dear Sister,

Just a few lines tonight to let you know I am still alive and well and hope this will find you all the same.

We have been pretty busy the last few weeks, but the weather is dark and cold so it put a damper on any very heavy fighting. I expect as soon as it clears up they will be at it harder than ever. You would think to look at the map that Fritz was walking over us but he is paying a horrible price for every yard taken and the country they are going through is only a wilderness of mud so if he can't do any better that he has done there is no need to worry.

I had the misfortune to smash my watch the other night and as it would take nearly six months in England to have it repaired, I am going to send it to you and have it fixed right which I think is the quickest and best. So when you get the bill will you send it to Hattie for she is paying any little debts for me. I certainly feel lost without it for it keeps the best of time and there are very few in the Battery.

I had a letter from Lewis Drake* last week. He is over here but is stationed quite a distance from me, so it's not likely I will see him for some time.

I suppose they are lining the boys up around there. What about Tim? Will he have to come?

Well I have no news, so will close hoping this finds you all well.

Yours lovingly,
Arthur

---

* Possibly Louis Drake (2115060) born in Cornwall, PEI, December 1888. A carpenter who joined up at Winnipeg in March 1917.

THE ONE HUNDRED DAYS:
AUGUST 8 - NOV 11, 1918

Arthur Harrison
No. 13 Canadian Field Ambulance, France

September 1, 1918

Dear Mother,

As I have not written a letter for over a month I will scribble an answer to yours which I received some time ago. I have received about twenty letters which I have not had the opportunity to answer. As it is, you will have to pass this around as I cannot write any more until I have a more favourable opportunity.

I have been keeping quite well right along until today, but I just have a little stomach trouble. I have been through H_ _l these last thirty days but here I am not much the worse for it. Now mother I don't think you expect a very long letter from me under these conditions.

Well how is everything going home? Has Warden and Willie* been called up yet? Mother don't think that I have forgotten you because I don't write. I send a letter in Gladys's name for the whole of you. I suppose Lizzie has gone home now. Mother, don't look for many letters from me for quite a while yet. I will close now because you don't get any letters from me do not fail to write.

Your affectionate son,
Arthur

---

* Warden was Arthur's older brother born in 1888 and William, Arthur's younger brother by one year, was born in 1898.

Charles McInnes
CRT, *France*

October 20, 1918

My dear girl,

*O*ur home just now is not just as comfortable as the other one was, but the place is just as quiet. No bombing or shelling around us at all. We are about forty miles from the front line. I do not know how long we will be here, but there is a lot of work to do. They are advancing so fast that the railway troops cannot keep up with them. But I expect some of these fine days we will get up as near the front line as we want to. The war news last week was grand but we cannot expect it to be as good this week. No need to say anything of war news for you folks know more and hear more than we do. And by the time my letter reaches you the news I would write would be as stale as could be. But I hope it will be over this year... Last week there was three mines blew up. No one was hurt and did not do much—an awful lot of damage to the track. It takes fifty men and four teams of mules with scrapers four days to fill one of the holes. That will give you some idea how large the holes are...

Yes, over two years have gone now since I left home and

Charles McInnes's girls, Mary, Orlo, and Margaret.

looking back it does not seem so long and we have a mighty lot to be thankful for...But it makes me sad when I think of all the boys who have come over in the last two years and a good many will never return. But it is all for a good cause. And their past is not one of shame. I only wish it was the Germans who were filling in fast in the place of all the boys who have been fighting on our side. I've got no use for a German and hope I never will have, for I have seen too much and heard so much of their dirty work. You have no idea what they will do... If I do not have to work Sunday I am going to take a walk over the grounds where the fighting has been so severe; am anxious to see that wonderful trench system the Germans had. Now I am about through for this time, so I guess I will stop. With love to all, as ever, yours,
    Chas

VIEWS ON CONSCRIPTION

Canada's willing participation in the First World War created unexpected and unforeseen challenges and crises for the country as a whole. No one had expected the war to last so long and to cost so many lives and for there still to be no end in sight even in 1917. New battalions were broken up for reinforcements and still there were not enough men. Ironically, after the great victory of Vimy Ridge in April 1917 it became obvious that both the rate and number of men volunteering was insufficient to sustain Canada's war effort. The federal Unionist government of Robert Borden was forced to opt for conscription.

    The bitter conscription election of December 1917 pitted French Quebecers against English Canada and rural against urban. However, in New Brunswick, the significant Acadian population were of a different mind and had raised an infantry battalion of their own, the 165th. Furthermore, in the Maritimes, differences between rural farmers and fishermen on the one hand and city dwellers on the other were not so clearcut—most families had significant rural ties. The Maritimes had another element in the mix which many other parts of the nation did not—a long history of being here. Many Canadians were first-generation immigrants with recent ties to the old world and a war there drew them back. Most Maritimers had been here for generations. The men and women serving overseas voted overwhelmingly in favour of conscription.

The following letters reflect several concerns. Have other family members been called up? Often those serving viewed themselves as their family's contribution. Some of the men expected their family to vote against conscription for some men had to be left at home to run the farm. While understanding this, Art Drake wonders what folks were thinking—would they prefer German rule? Jay and his friends stress that a distinction had to be made and maintained in the public mind between those who volunteered and served in the war zone and those who were conscripted. Finally, Fred Morell expresses the fairly common view that conscripted men would neither be welcomed in the ranks nor were they likely to be very good soldiers—having been forced into it after all. In practice, both worries failed to materialize.

Arthur Harrison
13th Canadian Field Ambulance, France

December 7, 1917

Dear Father,

As I have a little while to myself I will write you a short letter to tell you that I am enjoying good health. I just received a letter from Gladys [sister] the other day but I have not had time to answer it yet.

Has anything been said about Will or Warden[*] being called up for military service yet? If they are called up and cannot come, just send

---

[*] Arthur's brothers; Warden born in 1888 and William born in 1898.

me a cable gram. Write and tell me about the election around there. I expect everybody there voted against conscription. Just like them I have to write short letters over here, so you fellows will have to do all the writing. I hope everybody is well around there. How much snow is there yet? There hasn't been any here yet, and I suppose when it does come it will soon turn into water to make the roads muddy—that seems to be always the case. Well I will close for this time so write and tell me all the news as soon as you get this.

Yours respectfully,
Arthur

Arthur William Drake
France

February 4, 1918

Dear Sister,

I received your very welcome letter last week, and as I have a little time to myself I thought I would drop you a line.

I have been up at the guns ever since coming from Blighty and expect to stay for a few weeks longer if all goes well and Fritz don't get me scared out, for he is throwing a few around once in a while to keep us on the move.

Well, we are having the best winter weather I have ever seen, so far very little cold or rain and plenty of bright sunny days like the later part of April at home. If it will only keep up we will have no room to kick. I told you in my last letter about seeing Harry McGregor* and was asking about other boys from home, but I wouldn't know any as

---

* Harry McGregor (7125657) born in Cornwall, PEI, 1896 and joined the 105 Battalion in January 1916.

everybody has changed. The ones that I used to know at home are scattered or married and any that are out here have grown up since I was home. I wouldn't have known Harry if he hadn't come and spoken to me.

I notice PEI didn't give conscription very much of a help. What was the trouble? Would they sooner live under German rule?

Are there any of the boys around there being called up? What about Tim, they can't surely take him.

Well, there is nothing more I can write you so will close. Hoping you are all well as this leaves me feeling fine.

Yours truly,
Arthur

Ed E. Jay
26th Battalion, France

October 25, 1918

Dear Mother & All,

*A*s I have a few minutes to spare this evening I will pen you a few lines. I hope you are all well and happy. As for Ted, he is feeling fine and quite happy, especially this evening. I just got a can with two cakes in it, and Oh! what a feed I had. I gave Fred a piece, and Lyman* is coming in to spend a few minutes with me tonight and I will give him some too. I gave all my chums that are with me some and they all send many thanks, and for Ted sending thanks you know how pleased I am. You also know how I would thank you people for your kindness, if I could just drop in for a few minutes, but for now I send many thanks. I do not deserve all these nice parcels.

I must write Maggie a line tonight too, as it is a long time since I wrote to her. I hope she will get along OK. I am very glad it is a little

---

* Possibly Lyman V. Jay (3204093) born in Fanning Brook, PEI, 1893.

girl for if 'twas a boy, I would be frightened he would perhaps be in the army in a few years, "ha ha." I guess though, there is not much chance of the war lasting that long by the way it is going. The news seems to be pretty good now and we are very busy so that is why I don't write more often, and don't expect will very regular for a while, but I will do my best to write. I will try to send a field card if I don't write. My hand is perfectly well again. I suppose by the time you get this note you will be beginning to prepare for Christmas—just think, two months from today. I wonder what will be the news by then from "A Coy 26th Batt, Canadian, B.E.F. France*." Does Lyman's people worry much about him? He is quite well so far.

I received a letter from Hazel⁺ last week with a slip she cut out of the paper about that memorial service which was held in our church. It was very nice indeed, but listen well: I don't mean that I am any better than the other boys who are just enlisting, but I was talking to Lorne Jay* and Fred Smith and some more boys from around our place who voluntarily enlisted and they all seem to think that on this honour roll and other places that our names appear that there should be some distinction shown between the boys who voluntarily joined the army and the ones that are called up. I think it is perfectly right too, for there are names on that roll of boys that I am doubtful if they left PEI yet. And people will give them just as much credit as the ones who are over in France two or three years for the simple reason that they think that they are in France and they don't deserve the credit at all.

You take and consider that yourself. We are no better than they are, but we put in harder times than they will ever know. So they will make some sort of distinction between those boys and us before I ever look at that roll.

- In other words, what will the news be from his battalion in two months.
- Hazel, Edward's older sister, born 1892.
- Possibly Lorne M. Jay (713016) born 1898 at Pisquid, PEI, joined 105 Battalion in March 1916.

I guess it is about time I was writing Maggie a letter and sending my love to all, and to you and to all my friends, "May God bless you all."

I remain, your loving son,

Eddie

Fred Morell
Glasgow

March 10, 1918

Dear Mother,

I intended to write you ever since I came over on leave, but I have been on the go pretty steady and just managed to write to Grace [his wife] now and then. I am going back to London tonight, and am just waiting now until it is time to go to the station. I have until Wednesday morning before I go back to France, so I will have a chance in London to get a few things that I want to take back with me. Well, I have enjoyed my stay here very much, although I wasn't feeling at all well when I left France. I am OK now, and wish I could stay here for about a month, but, of course, I am one of the fools in khaki. I don't suppose you like to hear me say that, as you are an upholder of conscription, I am sorry to learn. However, we won't fall out on that account. Well I suppose by the time you get this you will have seen the winter over and be enjoying some spring weather. We have had a fairly good winter in France, so I foresee a wet dirty spring. Now I must close for this time, but will write you as soon as I get back to the land of shell holes and barbed wire. Now don't worry about any of us, for I don't really think we will have it very terrible this year, but of course, one never knows. Remember me to Aunt Jessie and John Wilson and tell Jim that I will write to him.

With love,

Fred

NURSES

Men were not the only Maritimers to serve overseas in the First World War. Nursing sisters, so called whether they were in religious orders or not, also served at hospitals in England as well as in France and Belgium. Ina Lockhart, from the village of Petiticodiac, a graduate of Newton Hospital in Massachusetts, USA served in France and Belgium. Her letters make for very interesting reading. Her excitement at travelling, of seeing new sights in England, of meeting new people, of doing her bit for the war effort—her sense of liberation comes across in her letters very clearly. Her joy at seeing boys from around home, that is, from Petitocidiac, NB, is also clear. Her words about accepting the death of her brother Frank and her advice to her mother upon her youngest brother also joining up are most telling. Although brimming with life and joy, her cold calculations about better to be dead than maimed like many she had nursed, make for stark reading indeed. Clearly, nurse Ina Lockhart had seen her share of the results of twentieth-century technological warfare.

Nursing Sister Ina Lockhart
France

January 31, 1917

Dear Mrs. Jones,

*H*ere it is the 31st of January and almost two months since I have been on active service. We have no difficulty in keeping busy—consequently time for letter writing is very limited.

To go back to the time we started which was November 20th from New York, I shall give you a brief outline of my trip.

We had a perfectly splendid trip across. The weather was perfect, not a bad day on the whole trip. The ocean is beyond one's imagination. I greatly enjoyed the sunsets, and got up almost every AM to see sunrise, which sight I shall never forget. I was real sick the first two days out. Got out on deck, but the smell of beef tea upset me, and I was unable to sit up. Lived on arrowroot and ginger ale for two days. The third day out I was just fine.

We played shuffleboard and throw about every day on deck, and the evenings were spent in the reception room. I got into trouble the first night by playing for them to dance—after that I could not get out of it anyway—but of course I didn't mind, it always does me good to see others having a good time. And occasionally we sang all the good old songs that everyone knew. It was nice. Some fairly good singers among the passengers.

Nurse Ina Lockhart.

We had a day of sports, which we shall never forget. One of the doctors chose a Miss Jordan and I for leaders. Each had ten girls and the doctors were our judges. Mr. White (manager of the unit) started us in each race. We made out an immense programme inviting all the passengers and officers of the *Andania**. Needless to say, as many came as could get there. We met on the port side of the ship between 10:00 AM and 12:00 noon. Had a potato race, three-legged race, sack race, boot race, running, jumping, etc. We were tied until the tug-of-war, which came

---

* RMS *Andania*, a steamship sunk later on in the war by German submarine U-46 on January 27, 1918.

PART FOUR : THE REALITY OF WAR

last. We laughed so we couldn't stand up, consequently they simply dragged us the length of the deck. My side were all small girls. So we were called bantams. The others were called international champions. Miss Jordan got an elegant three-pound box of chocolates, while I got a beautiful basket of fruit, with a bunch of violets tied to the handle. It was really very nice. It's one day none of us will ever forget. The same day I climbed to the top of the wireless forty or fifty feet above the top deck. One of the doctors went with me. It was great.

We landed at Plymouth, but I must tell you more of our good times on board. You see we were a small unit, so the officers and doctors certainly made it very pleasant for us. The chief engineer had us for 4:00 PM tea and showed us all the machinery of the boat, which I greatly enjoyed. I put a shovel of coal on one of the furnaces. Then the purser and his assistant, two fine chaps, had us—Mae, Ann, and I—for tea, also the ship's doctor. Certainly it was very nice, and we appreciated their hospitality very much indeed. It was not only once but on several occasions.

We arrived at Plymouth the 30th November, and went from there to London by train. A tired bunch we were when we arrived around 9:00 PM. Did not have to be sung to sleep, I can assure you.

We just had one week at London, but a wonderful week it was. We visited the Tower, Parliament buildings, House of Commons and Lords, and magnificent Westminster Abbey is too beautiful. We went to a Sunday service at Westminster Abbey, also at St. Paul's Cathedral. The chanting and music were wonderful. We walked across London Bridge, saw old Southwick Cathedral…

We saw the museum, Buckingham Palace when the guards were being changed. Very pretty and most interesting. The war office is a huge place. Whitehall, Pall Mall, and the Marble Arch, Hyde Park.

I called on Mr. Fred Sumner of Moncton. You know he is the agent general for New Brunswick. He is fine. Let us have his auto and chauffeur for some time. We, of course, saw lots that we could not have seen otherwise.

You know Will and Harry* of the 104th were transferred from Shorncliffe to Witley Camp while we were on the ocean, so I spent a day with them. Saw all the home boys—and certainly those poor youngsters were glad to see someone from home. They all looked well and were much more comfortable in the huts than they had been before in the tents. They hired an auto, so we had a memorable day. The country is beautiful. Holly hedges, ivy, and plenty of green grass then.

Mr. and Mrs. Hall, friends of Frank's✢, came to the hotel to see me, took me to the theatre, and I also spent the day with them at their home at Gravesend. They took me for an auto ride through Dickens country... I can understand why Kent is called the Garden of England. Parts of it are beautiful. We passed old thatched houses and I can't tell you how I enjoyed it. They even took me to where poor Frank and his men dug trenches when stationed at Sandling.

We left London the 8th December. Got here the evening of the 8th. Had a good trip across the channel and spent some time in Boulogne. We went on duty the AM of the 9th and have been on the go ever since.

The patients are all in large tents and huts. I can't tell you anything except that we hear pitiful stories, and one's heart aches for them. They are splendid fellows and more than appreciate a word from a woman.

We are all in huts, ten or twelve nurses in each hut and two girls in each room. We have cots, two chairs, two tables, a very small stove and a shelf was donated to us. We have packing boxes with shelves in them for our clothes and pantry, etc. So with some pine, holly, and even mistletoe up on the wooden walls, with our calendars and Christmas cards, we are quite cosy. I do wish you could see us.

It was perfect on the boat, perfect in London, but Mrs Jones, it rained every single day since we arrived, until about ten days ago, and it's been very cold.

---

* Ina's brothers William Rufus Lockhart (709679) and Harry Ray Lockhart (709579), who both joined the 104 NB Battalion at Sussex on November 1, 1915.

✢ Ina's older brother, Lieutenant Frank E. Lockhart of the 26th NB Battalion, missing since the previous April and presumed dead.

PART FOUR : THE REALITY OF WAR

Really, I never saw so much rain and mud in my life. It was awful. Rain hats, coats, and rubber boots all the time, but I love the work.

Of course the extreme dampness has been terribly hard on us all. Some of the girls have been off, ill with bad colds, etc. Mine is all better. I'm feeling fine.

The food is plain, but tastes great. I have gained and look better than I have looked for some time.

We had a nice Christmas—even cranberry sauce. The boys had a very nice Christmas too. We decorated the tents with pine, holly, ivy, and green and red crepe paper. The boys were delighted. We sang carols. Some of those fellows were splendid singers, and we all had a very merry day. We worked hard but were happy to know we helped in a way different from other years—and while I never had so little, it was the best 25th I ever had—the most satisfactory...

Ina Lockhart

Nursing Sister Ina Lockhart
London, England

June, 1917

Dearest Mother and Dad,

I am not surprised to learn of Bob's signing up[*], for I knew that he meant to. I'm sorry, but admire him, and mother it's more to his credit than to stay home. Try to bear up, and realize that it's an honourable thing, even though it is sad. Surely they won't all be killed and if they are, what could they do that would be any better? We can only hope that before he sees France, the thing will have stopped, and

---

[*] Ina's younger brother, Robert Earl Lockhart (2303891) joined the No. 2 NB Forestry Company CEF on May 21, 1917, at the age of seventeen years and nine months.

speaking of Frank, Will, and Harry—mother I am trying to think that Frank is dead. I would much rather they would all be killed, than wounded like some of the boys are, and allowed to live.

If you could see what we have seen since coming to London, you could understand why I write this. It's pathetic beyond words. Do try to look at it in the right way and be glad they are fit to do their bit whatever that may be. I am proud to see my brother's name in "Canada in Flanders," one of the greatest battles that was ever fought; Ypres, St. Eloi, and Sanctuary Woods. There are two volumes written by Lord Beaverbrook and Frank is mentioned—Arthur Moore[*] sent me the book only yesterday.

You can't imagine how glad I was to see him. He is a Lieutenant now—elegant, big, fine-looking and splendid fellow. We talked a blue streak, and he is taking me to "Hampton Court" Monday and to the theatre in the evening. We had such a nice time. I am the first Petitcodiacer he has seen in the form of a woman, and he was glad to see me. We had the most gorgeous time at Lord and Lady Desborough's. I think I told you all about the wonderful place—we went through Windsor Castle and Eaton College and enjoyed a six-mile trip on the river Thames every AM. Had some elegant games of lawn tennis with both Lord and Lady D. Also the young daughter twelve or thirteen years old—the honourable Imogene—a sweet thing.

One day we had a lovely picnic out under some gorgeous old tress and another day she entertained some convalescent soldiers. We had the nicest time, and mind you a couple of them had come from the 22nd General—rather funny, wasn't it?[*]

We just came up to London Tuesday and this is Friday. We hope to go to Scotland and expect to have a week or ten days there, while we are getting uniforms, etc. finished. I expect to stay here as long as

---

[*] Arthur Charles Moore (435022) born in Petticodiac, unmarried and joined the 50th (Calgary) Battalion in March 1915.

[*] This was the hospital Ina worked at in England.

PART FOUR : THE REALITY OF WAR

I feel perfectly well. Please do not worry about me for I'm real well. I weigh 113 pounds and am so glad mother dear, that I can help too. So do take care of yourself and just think how much I shall have to tell you and just now I want to see you so much.

I know those flowers must be pretty. Be sure you don't work outside unless your feet are well protected and something on your head, for I don't want to hear of you not being well. I should like to have the chance to dig around those old rose bushes myself. Oh mother, do have a vine of some kind around that tree that was killed just in front of the house—they grow quickly and look so pretty around the trunk. They have them here everywhere and are just lovely.

I shall not write any more now so hope that those letters reached you alright. Much love to you all—got a box of four pounds maple sugar and four chocolate bars from Mrs. Fleming and a long, long letter from Mona—write me soon.

Love to Elsie and yourselves and do get Bob to have some pictures taken in uniform—bless his heart. Just had a letter from Jack Blakney—he is getting on well. Bye, bye,

Ina

PART FIVE

The End Has Come

THE WAR IS OVER

For gootness sake go back Here kom der **CANADIANS**.

A humorous cartoon from 1916.

The Armistice which ended hostilities came into effect at 11:00 am on November 11, 1918. Canadians fought right up to the very end. Fred Morell tells of his battery firing until dark on the 10th and then moving the guns forward in order to resume firing on the 11th. Both Fred and Art Harrison ended their war just outside the Belgian city of Mons where the British retreat had begun four years earlier. All men relate that the soldiers took the news quietly. At first, it was hard to believe, and some didn't. With the guns silenced, there was much to reflect upon. Fred regretted the loss of his brother Horace. George Chapman looked forward to returning home to Cape Breton. First, however, there was the need to occupy Germany to ensure compliance with the terms of the Armistice. Ed Jay was one of the Canadian soldiers who, in spite of an injury, marched into Germany. He shared some pointed thoughts with the folks at home upon learning of Germany's hesitation to sign off on the terms. These matters would take time. At the time of the Armistice and for months to come, the Belgian population greeted the Canadians as the conquering heroes they actually were. The German occupation had been long, stern, and difficult.

Fred Morell
Belgium

November 15, 1918

Dear Mother,

Just a few lines today while I am in the mood for writing to let you know that I am still well and that the prospects of remaining so are good. Although the fighting is finished we will not be sent home for a while; how long I have no idea. We expect to start one of these days on the march into Germany, and I don't suppose things will be fixed up officially until we get there. That will take us three weeks or a month at the rate we are supposed to travel. At present we are near Mons, the city that the British retreat started from in the fall of 1914. Yesterday afternoon I was all over the city taking in the sights and visited all the places of interest. It is a grand city and well worth seeing, being one of the most historic places on the continent. I can't begin to describe it to you now but will be able to tell you all about it when I get home. The people, wherever we go, give us a royal welcome and seem to think that they can't do enough for us. When we pulled into the city with our guns last Monday, that was the day that the Armistice started, I never saw such a happy, highly excited crowd, or never expect to. We were received in a "Hail the conquering hero comes" manner and I would not have missed being there for anything. It was an experience I will never forget and for the first time since coming to France, was proud that I was in the Canadian army and up the line when the Huns threw up the sponge.

It was hard to realize for a few days that the war was really over and that the last shot had been fired. The day before the word came through we had been in action until about dark, and then pulled our guns further up, in fact to the outskirts of Mons, never dreaming that we were through, and when the communiqué came through the next morning to stand fast, we thought it was a huge joke, but I haven't heard the sound of a gun since, and I sincerely hope that I never will again.

PART FIVE : THE END HAS COME

This trek to Germany will no doubt be a long, tiresome one, but at that it will be better than the hardships and uncertainties of fighting. I for one have had enough narrow escapes, and seen enough bloodshed to do me for the rest of my days and I am thankful that I will not have any more such experiences.

I wish Horrie* had been lucky enough to stick it out for a few more months, but it doesn't do to think too much about the things that had to be. Now I must close for this time, as it is just about noon, but I will write again when I can. Probably when we are on the march there won't be much time unless we halt for a day occasionally. Remember me to all the folks.

Lovingly,
Fred

George T. Chapman
85th Battalion, Somewhere in France

November 9, 1918

Dear Mary,

Well, how are you Mary? I am fine. Say, this 'ere blinkin war will soon be over won't it? They say that by Monday morning we will know whether old Fritz is going to throw up the sponge or stand a few more rounds. But one way or the other, he cannot stand the pace that we are lambasting him at the present time. We have got his number and intend to keep it for good…

⁺Say Mary, I had to quit working the other night and by this time we know that old Fritz has accepted our terms of the Armistice. That means that he is down and out. He will sign the peace terms now and

---

* Horace Morell, Fred's younger brother, was killed August 8, 1918, at the start of the Hundred Days.

⁺ Picks up several days later.

the general opinion is that we have seen the last of the fighting.

You will likely want to know how the troops behaved when they heard that the Armistice was signed. I was told at 9:00 on Monday morning that it was official—that it was signed, and I had to then proceed about six kilometers along on duty, so I just watched the troops at the different places I passed. There was no excitement shown, it was all taken in a very matter-of-fact way although there was a happy expression on all the faces you looked at. In fact, we cannot realize that the last shot may have been fired and we pinch ourselves once in a while to see if we are not living in a dream but...we are awake alright, alright!

However, one task is still cut out for us for a little time, and that is to see that he conforms to the Armistice that he has signed. We are entering a very novel part of the war and it sure is going to be interesting. So I'm thinking that I should have plenty of matter to write of within the next few weeks; that is, if they lift the censorship regulations which they no doubt will as soon as they get things in shipshape order.

Must thank you very much for that nice box of cake and fudge. It landed when we could not get many luxuries as Fritz had requisitioned all the civilians possessed and our canteens had not much of a selection to pick and choose from.

Remember me to all my old friends and tell them that I hope it will not be so very many months before the old ship sails home. I feel as fit as a fiddle, so am in good form for the return journey whenever they order it that way.

Am writing this note in a beautiful home—whoever owned this must have been worth all kinds of money. Have an open grate with a peach of a fire on and a nice comfortable easy chair. Who said the soldiers were not well off?

Well I think I'll ring off for the present. Remember me to all the folks. Kindest regards and best wishes.

Sincerely yours,
George

PART FIVE : THE END HAS COME

Arthur Harrison
Havre, Belgium

November 26, 1918

Dear Sister,

It gives me great pleasure to answer your letters of 8, 16, and 27 of October which I received yesterday when I got back off leave. I am now just outside of Mons at a little village called Havre. Am having a tip-top time here. It is some change to hear no guns. The people here will do anything in their power for us; they praise the Canadians greatly. One could not find people more hospitable anywhere. It is a very pretty country here, and none of the towns are torn to pieces much. It is a pity though to see the people coming back from the German lines with big loads on their backs or on wagons and wheelbarrows or whatever they can get trudging along to their homes which a great many of them will find in ruins.

I expect to have a trip to the Belgian capital (Brussels) before I go back across the ocean to Canada. There are quite a bunch of the boys going. I only hope I am lucky enough to get there.

Tell Bill I got the photo; it was very nice. I could not recognize the tree he is sitting on. I had some photos taken in London, but have not received them yet, but when they come, if they are any good, I will send you some. Tell Will* there is no fear of him being called up now as the job is finished and by the time you get this, peace will be declared and perhaps I will be on my way to Halifax. But it may be March or April before I can get home as there are so many soldiers to go back that it will be some time before we are all out of France.

Oh yes, I got two boxes and the contents were delicious. I nearly made myself sick eating. I sent mother a 4 Canadian Division magazine

---

* Art's younger brother William, born 1898.

which I hope you will like. I would like to send you a nice Christmas present, but I missed my seventy-franc pay and it would take all of that to buy anything any good. I would love to get some Flemish lace but that costs about one hundred Francs (twenty dollars) a yard so you see it takes money to buy things out here. Now I am going to close and get to bed. Hope to hear from you again very shortly.

N.B. About all we are doing now is shining up for inspections.

Ta ta.

Your loving brother,
Arthur

Edward E. Jay
26th Battalion, France

February 16, 1919

Dear Mother,

Today I received a letter from you dated January 12th, also a note from papa and a dollar which I must thank him very much for, also had a letter the other day dated January 9th. I do love to get letters from you people, but it's really funny about my mail going to you people, but you know when we were on the march to Germany it was not very convenient to write for over three weeks. We would march in day and rest at night, so one could not write very well, but as soon as I got settled down in Germany, I wrote a lot of letters.

Now in my last letter I promised to tell you what I am doing away from the battalion. Well, tell the truth, I am in a hospital but don't start to worry til I tell you what is to matter with me. You know my poor weak foot? Well, on my march to Germany, oh, my God I suffered, but would not give in. After I got there I was laid up for a week, my foot all swollen up. When it started to get better, I would walk on my heel for a good while and I suppose as you would well imagine the tendons behind my knee also caused a small lump to come on my left joint. As I paid no attention to this sore lump so it went on from day to day. At last I got lame from it, so I reported it to the doctor. Oh, he said, that was nothing, "carry on." Finally, my whole leg began to swell, so then the doctor said, better go to hospital. On January 20th I came here. I was a bed patient for about two weeks, 'til the swelling all went away. Now I am up around but not allowed to walk much. I feel fine though. I said when I came here to one of the sisters that I would not send word home and she said no it would only cause you worry, but now that I am well again I will tell you. I will likely get back with our bunch. Now for God's sake don't worry for I am alright and in perfect care. Those Canadian nurses are just like angels to us, but you send my mail still to the battalion as I will be going out of here in at least two weeks time. I hear from Bella every second day but don't mention anything to her…

It was a very mild winter over here. I see by the paper that Germany don't seem willing to sign the peace terms, damn them. One should start it up again and bombard the devil out of the towns—civilians and all. Now I will close, but I will write Wednesday and Sunday regular. The little nurse who attends on me is from Toronto. She is beside me now and sends her best regards. She is over here three years. We were out for a walk and to church service together this morning. She is just like a real sister. She says when we all get back to our homes she is coming to PEI for a visit. I will close. Same address as usual. Best love to all. Thanks to papa. Bye, bye,

from Eddie

The 1916 Christmas card of the 26th New Brunswick Battalion.

WAITING TO GO HOME

Once the war was over everyone wanted to get home as soon as possible. The troops had, however, been ferried across the Atlantic over the course of four years, so getting them all home would take time. Both Ed Jay and Art Harrison made comments on the decided order of return—Art can accept that he has to wait as a member of the camc, but Jay is impatient. Fred Boehner, by contrast, is contented. Wounded outside Cambrai on October 18, he is healing well and looks forward to a week of leave in Scotland. Understandably, the men's thoughts also turn to the future. Ed Jay thinks he'll head out west. He was the stubborn one who enlisted, while his two brothers who stayed at home, in his words, deserve to get the two family farms. Ed Jay clearly had no thoughts of veteran entitlement! He signs off as "Daddie's Blockhead." Ominously, Art Harrison makes mention of admitting five new cases of the "flu"—the pandemic had begun. Ed Jay also makes mention of "the next war which I believe will be soon" although he does not elaborate as to just why he has such dark thoughts.

PART FIVE : THE END HAS COME

Fred Boehner
161st Battalion
Canadian General Hospital, Kent

January 7, 1919

Dear Mother and Father,

This is Tuesday noontime and I am in the ward writing this. I am going on leave today to Scotland and then I am returning to our discharge depot at Buxton, so it seems that I will be home before long. It is raining now but hope it clears up before long. I am sending you a few postcards taken here on Christmas Day and hope you will like them. Please do not send me any more boxes as I may not be here in England for long. I received your Christmas boxes and everything was great. In no. 2 picture I am the fellow with a white spot which was caused by light shining on my check. I am well and hope you are the same. Must close now, love to all,

Fred

Ed E. Jay
26th Battalion, France

January 31, 1919

Dear Momma,

Hope this note will find you all well as it leaves me the same. Guess it is pretty cold down on PEI—it is cold here but no snow, just nice clean weather. I suppose some of the boys are arriving home before this. I hear they are sending the ones home first that enlisted

first, but that is not fair because some who enlisted in 1915 and came over to England stayed there for a long time and just came to France for a few months will get back first, ahead of men even like myself who enlisted in April 1916, and now have just two years straight in France. They should send them home by the time they served in France. But anyway, if I get home before next fall I will be satisfied. I don't think I will be home for long. I have a notion to go out west after I get a little rest. There will be just the two farms, home for Ollie and Harry*, so it will be up to Ted to keep on travelling. They are the ones who deserve it too. They stayed at home and helped their parents, wherein Ted did not. He got stubborn and enlisted, although I would take their place for the past three years, if one had them to live over again. But forget that til we get a chance to talk or debate on it. But anyway, Eddie Boy was one of those that would never make anything and perhaps he didn't, but I don't fancy a war life now. Someone else will have to come the next war, which I believe will be soon. I guess I better close, will write soon again. Remember me to all around. Best love to you all, I am the same,
    Daddies's Blockhead,
    Ted

Arthur Harrison
CAMC, *Bramshott, England*

March 29, 1919

Dear Mother,

I will write you a short letter today hoping it will find you in good health and spirits. I am still working in hospital and do not yet

---

* Edward's older (Oliver b. 1887) and younger (Harold b. 1897) brothers, respectively.

PART FIVE : THE END HAS COME

see any prospects of my early return to Canada, although I have good reason to believe it will not be too many more months before I will be there. You see the medical corps will be the last to be demobilized. That's why I am in this country so long. If I was in the infantry I should have been home long ago. The "flu" is raging around here too. I have just admitted five cases into hospital with it. I hope it is not serious there. It is queer that doctors cannot find what causes it. I seen in the papers that a French specialist discovered the germ, but it is hard to say if it is so. I had a touch of it when I was up in London on pass and barely escaped going to hospital with it.

Well mother, I suppose you are still at the old job feeding pigs and milking cows. How is father this spring? I suppose he is busy in the sugar woods now. Well, I may be lucky enough to get there on the wind-up just in time to gather cans. I suppose sugar will be high this spring again. Now I must close as there is a fellow going out to the post office and I can get this mailed. Be sure and write again soon. Your loving son,
    Art

LAST LETTER HOME

The wait to actually get on board a ship for home was longer than expected. By February 1919, Fred Boehner is at a camp in Wales meeting other men from the Bridgewater area and sounding quite content. Ed Jay by contrast, although an infantryman also, still finds himself in Belgium a month after Fred wrote his people. Ed Jay is understandably impatient. Art Harrison, the camc man who knew he would be later than others getting back, writes while recovering in hospital from tonsillitis. It was by then mid-May 1919—a full six months after war's end!

Fred Boehner
161st Battalion
Rhyl, Wales

February 16, 1919

Dear Mother and Father,

For a wonder the army has moved a little quick for once and I arrived here from Witley last night—it was about a ten-hour trip on the train and we were all glad when we landed here as we were all very hungry. Well, what we have to do here now is to wait until our name is called out for the boat and do fatigues. I hope they don't take very many days before they call mine out. Well, I had quite a surprise the other evening—I met Cushing* from Bridgewater who used to be in the 219th. Also another lad from Yarmouth, he was home from France on leave and looked well. We spent the evening together, but he had to go back the same night and today I met Ink Wile⁺. He is waiting here the same as myself, so I may go back on the same boat as he does. It is quite foggy here today. Hope you are all well, must close, love to all from,
    Fred.

P.S.: Please do not write any more letters as they do not reach me and I may be back before they arrive.

- Alexander Burton Cushing (282294) born 1898 in Bridgewater and joined the 185th Battalion there in March 1916.
- Daniel Inkerman Wile (282287) born at Lahave, NS, in 1873 and joined 219 Battalion at Bridgewater in March 1916.

PART FIVE : THE END HAS COME

Ed E. Jay
26th Battalion, Belgium

March 19, 1919

My dear Mamma,

I suppose you think Ted is lost but no I am still with the 26th Battalion. I thought we were going to England when I wrote last, that is the reason I said for you not to write again 'til you hear from me again, but I don't think we will be going till the first week in April. That will let us get home about the middle or last of May. Oh rot, what a long time to wait, but it will be good when it does come, although we are having a good time here, just like home, at least I make myself at home anyway. I am staying with a man and a woman and little girl ten years old in a town called Lamines, Belgium, quite a nice little town. We are having lovely weather here now, just like May down home. You said in one of your letters that I would be home for to help put out the nets, but my darling mom I don't think I will. But what odds I would not work anyway just sport around. Oh, what we will have! You say there are some boys returning; a credit to some, a disgrace to others. I wonder what I will be—a credit or a disgrace? The latter I guess. I did not see Lyman* lately nor don't want to. Lorne Jay⁺ is gone home to be a military police in Truro. One thing, we will be arriving home in nice weather, drunk every day, "ha ha." I guess I will close. It is really too bad about Eliza. I worried when I heard it first, I cried some too, believe me. I am not too old or big to have that soft heart yet. I do hope you all keep well. Give my best love to all, will write a long letter to papa.

I remain, your loving son,
Eddie

---

* Possibly cousin Lyman Victor Jay (3204093) drafted November 27, 1917.
⁺ Another Islander, possibly cousin Lorne M. Jay (713016) born 1898, joined 105 Battalion in March 1916.

Arthur Harrison
CAMC, *Bramshott, England*

May 15, 1919

Dear Sister,

Have just been discharged from hospital today. I had a slight touch of tonsillitis. I have transferred back to the 13th Canadian Field Ambulance, and they attached me to the 44th Battalion for discharge. We expect to sail on the 27th of this month and if we do, will land in Canada about the 4th of June. The 44th Battalion goes to Moncton, but I am getting my discharge in Saint John and will have to go down there before I go home. I know there is a lot of red tape, but it will soon be over.

I got your letter dated April 25th, and it reminds me that I will soon be an old man (ha ha). Well Gladys, I don't know how I am going to fill in the twelve days before we will be going to Canada as it will seem like two months.

I am not working in "No. 4 Sick Detention Hut" any longer. But I will be able to get my mail all right. You had better not write any more letters to me, but I will write you quite often until we sail. And when I get to Halifax perhaps I can send you a telegram. So here's 'til I write again,

your loving brother, Art

P.S.: Tell Inez, Wilda, and Nathan* and others not to write to me anymore.

---

* Art's older sister, Inez, born 1890, his other sister, Wilda, born 1892 and married to Blake Marshall, and his older brother, Nathan, born 1884.

RAREST OF ALL – LETTERS FROM HOME

The soldiers overseas received many letters during the course of the war. Sometimes several family members wrote them weekly. Friends and other relatives also wrote. The men had no way to keep or store these letters—they could only keep what they could carry. The letters from home eventually had to be discarded.

This makes the following three letters unique. They reveal the toll the war was taking on the home front—the years of praying and hoping and waiting. In the first, Art Harrison's father, James, writes a letter to his son on a Sunday evening late in 1917. It survives on the reverse of an earlier letter, perhaps a draft, written to Art by his sister Ethel in October. The following two letters are to Waldo William Anderson of McKees Mills. Both were written on the same day, July 18, 1918. The first is written by Waldo's father Howard, the second by his sister Ethel. They were taken off Waldo's body by his chum, Arnold B. Wright, just after Waldo was killed on August 26th. Arnold gave them and Waldo's pocketbook to the company clerk to send back home. Arnold later wrote the family a letter explaining his actions.*

My dear boy Arthur,

*A*s this is Sunday night and they are all gone out to meeting but me and Lila and Olive, so it seems a bit lonesome.† I was just thinking about you and if you ever get lonesome and think of home. I know it makes my heart ache to think of you away out there and how I

---

* See above in the section entitled "On the Loss of a Friend."

† Delilah, born 1905 and Olive, born 1908.

wish and pray this awful war will soon be over so you can come home. They have conscription now and I expect some more of the men from around here will have to go. If so, it will be duller times than ever at home. On Sunday I seem to be alone all day, and they all went out to Sunday school; Warden and Glad* and baby went somewhere, Ira and Milford⁺ and the girls and Will come home but Will is so still he hardly ever speaks—it makes me sad to see him so.

Well, Art, I am feeling pretty well, only I have a queer headache in the mornings but I have to work away as hard as I can to get the work done as Glad is away quite a lot of the time. I have most all of the work to do. Ira is quite well this fall for him; I don't know how long it will last. He teamed the horses for Warden to plow the other day 'til he was tired out. Nathan* is well, Minnie is bothered with the asthma quite a lot this fall. The children are growing fine; Ella is a nice little mischief, you won't know her when you come home. Inez* and Charlie and the children are fine. Eva would sooner stay with me than home. Poor Wilda*, she don't get in home as often as she used to, and I feel very lonesome with not having her come. Blake has so much to do he can't take time to drive her in, and Edna is sick most all the time. Joe was up for two or three days—he seemed loath to go back, he said he wrote to you—don't forget to write to him... *[remainder of letter is missing]*

James W. Harrison

- Art's older brother, Warden, born in 1888 and older sister, Gladys, born in 1895.
- Art's younger brother, Milford, born in 1901.
- Art's older brother, Nathan, born in 1884.
- Art's older sister, Inez, born in 1890.
- Art's older sister, Wilda, born 1892 and married to Blake Marshall.

PART FIVE : THE END HAS COME

Howard Anderson
St. Anthony, NB

July 18, 1918

My dear son Waldo,

Ethel has written to you and so we are going to write and send in the same letter. We were much pleased to hear from you and to know that you were well. The first part of July was cold and wet, but we are getting warmer weather now, but frequent showers that make it difficult to cultivate and weed potatoes and garden. We did succeed in getting the turnips thinned and cultivated; also the potatoes have been gone over once. The crops are looking fairly well at present. If weather conditions are favourable there will be a fairly good harvest. The potato bugs are fairly swarming this summer. Harry Biggs and I bought a one-horse sprayer this week—we have got it and set it up, but have not used it yet, as the potatoes are scarcely large enough to spray yet. It will spray four rows at a time. We will use blue vitrol and lime with the Paris Green to prevent blight, and that will make a great difference in the yield of the potatoes as the stocks will keep green until the frost comes.

It will save a lot of hard work going up and down the rows with a sprinkling can. It costs $115 but I think it will pay for itself in one season. We are having a heavy thundershower today. The wheat is nearly ready to head out and the timothy is in blossom, and haying is here in less than two weeks by appearance now. Some of the new seeded ground will be a heavy cut. We were down to Buctouche last night and McLaughlin Co. are cutting some of their heavy clover—they will have an immense crop this year. I think we will have as much hay and perhaps more than last year. We wintered twelve head of cattle and three horses last winter and will have the barn full this winter. Will have to get rid of some before winter as we have sixteen head of cattle counting calves. We have an old sow and four young pigs. Feed is very high. Corn and corn meal is $4.00 per hundred and oats are $1.10 per bushel. On the other hand, eggs are worth 45¢ per dozen and butter 40¢ per pound. Potatoes are now $1.00 per bushel in Moncton. The old stock is about gone. We have only about six or eight bushels of potatoes to sell now. Have taken a lot out to Moncton this spring. Mamma and I were down to Middle Sackville to attend the grand division. We went out to Moncton Thursday morning, took a load of stuff out to sell, and went down to Sackville Thursday evening, and came back to Moncton Friday evening, finished selling on Saturday morning, and got home Saturday night. We had a very pleasant trip and enjoyed it very much.

Well dear boy, the war is still going on. I do hope and pray that it will end this year although I must confess I do not see much signs of it at present. We can only hope for the best. Praying the presence and divine protection of God for those engaged in this awful conflict. I must close for this time. Ethel has written about the news. From your affectionate father and mother,

W. H. & B. J. Anderson

Ethel (née Anderson)
McKees Mills, NB

July 18, 1918

Darling Brother,

We received two letters from you last week. The latest was written June 25th—we haven't had any word this week so far but are looking for a letter every night.

Well brother dear, how are you making out this warm weather? At least it is hot here. I don't know what it is like over there. I hope you are well as this leaves us. I see by the papers that there is another big battle going on now against the Americans, but I guess the Americans have held them so far. Colonel Rosevelt's son has been killed during the battle and likely there will be a good many more poor boys meet the same fate before the battle is over.

Fred Weldon and Howard McDonald were called up to report for duty at Sussex the 3rd of this month (July), but Howard didn't pass the medical exam, so he came back home, but Fred Weldon* passed so he has donned the khaki at last and is still at Sussex training but expects to go overseas in two or three weeks time. Mrs. Weldon was up to Sussex to see him last week. I would like to see him in khaki to see what he looks like but not likely I will as they never let the fellows come home. I don't think that is fair. John Farrell, Clarence Lesner, and Chas. Lesner have to report the first of November so that is the word they have now. I guess there won't be any fellows left on the river this winter. Ernest⁺ hasn't got any definite word yet but expects to get word to go any time. Everett is getting off very well for I don't think he has got any word yet. I don't think it will be fair if the rest of the boys has to go and he doesn't.

There is going to be another wedding the first of August; Edmund and Viola is going to get hitched up at last, it is about time isn't it? What do you think? I expect it will be some wedding. They are going to live in with Chas. Hicks for the present.

Our new minister has arrived. His name is Reverend John Lund, and he has a wife and three girls. He was here last Sunday for the first. I think he is going to be alright. They had a reception for him last night in the parsonage at Buctouche. There were only a few there but they had a good time. They are very nice in their own home.

Frank McDonald and his wife are living in Moncton now. She left him once for a little while but came back to him again. I tell you she has great love for him. Alice Ward and Mrs. Stanley are down here now that is all the Yankees there are yet, but I guess Bernice is coming before long.

---

* Fred E. Weldon (4061306) born 1895, of McKees Mills, NB.
⁺ Ethel's husband.

Well brother dear, I guess I will close for this time. Hoping to hear from you soon. How is that little Ethel of yours making out? I suppose you haven't seen her for some time. Will say goodbye for now, with heaps of love and kisses from all.

Your loving sister,
Ethel Grace

P.S.: Mrs. Will Cameron has a young daughter about two weeks old. Be sure and write often.

PART FIVE : THE END HAS COME

Afterword

The men who wrote these letters knew that the Great War was an extraordinary event, a terrible struggle of unparalleled proportions. They knew, to use the term they most often employed, that the war was *awful*. They did not, however, think it was pointless or needless. They felt it had to be fought. They had crossed the Atlantic to fight and kill Germans and there was a goal—to drive the German armies out of France and Flanders. The goal was to win the war and return home.

Edwin Goodwin of Baie Verte, NB, was a typical young Maritimer. He joined the 145th Infantry Battalion in 1916, but upon its breakup, served in the newly created Canadian Motor Machine Gun Brigade. Speaking to a high school class in 1982 he was asked why he volunteered. He had no hesitation in answering, "I joined up because I wanted to fight." Asked what was the sense of it all, he again replied immediately, "Canada had no choice; if Germany had won and defeated England and France—Canada itself would have been threatened."*

Germany had to be stopped, the war had to be fought. It's as if Vincent Goodwin had not heard of the conspiracy of the vast military-industrial complex, of the legions of useless, incompetent generals, and of the untold hordes of wasted young lives, but Vincent was an intelligent man and he had actually been there—for years. The view of the First World War which became predominant in the twentieth century and is now the conventional wisdom on the topic is not the view reflected in the letters of the men at the time. It was the creation of a segment of postwar writers who were predominantly English and university educated. Men who wrote and emoted well, writers and poets like Sassoon, Blunden, Graves, Remarque, and Owen. Their voices won the day and created the popular understanding of the Great War. They were not the only ones who wrote and reflected

---

* David P. Beatty, *Memories of the Forgotten War: The World War 1 Diary of Pte. V. E. Goodwin* (Baie Verte Editions, Saint John, 1989), xiv.

but far fewer know the name of the Englishman Sidney Rogerson* or know or read the memoirs of Vincent Goodwin from Baie Verte.

It's not that Sassoon and Owen got it all wrong, but it is high time for a reassessment of their perspective. Recently, historians like David Fromkin⁺ suggest that the Great War was a necessary and crucial step in bringing us to where we now are. The Western world is now a world of liberal democracies. One hundred years ago this was decidedly not the case. The German, Ottoman, Russian, and Austro-Hungarian empires did not vote themselves out of existence—they went out fighting. Those empires, those who ran them and the millions who lived under their immediate rule, were all ended and transformed as a direct result of the Great War. Further, as the European powers tore themselves apart, two other very significant trends began. First, the overlordship of their colonial empires began to come undone. As the century progressed, literally billions of people would gain their independence. Although the timeline was lengthier, this was even true for the winners, England and France. Secondly, the Great War witnessed a marked acceleration in the liberation of women in many of the countries involved. This is undeniably linked to their wartime injection into the workforce and their participation as nurses close to the front. Ina Lockhart's letters and the manner in which the wounded men refer to the nurses provide ample testimony to this change. In Canada, it was during the federal election of December 1917 when conscription was the issue, that the vote was extended to many women with a direct interest in the outcome. Following the war, despite opposition, the momentum to extend the franchise to women proved unstoppable. Women received the vote federally in Canada in 1919. Things did not proceed as quickly in other jurisdictions. For instance, in secular, republican France, women did not gain the vote until 1947.

---

* Sidney Rogerson, *Twelve Days on the Somme: A memoir of the Trenches, 1916* (Greenhill Books, London, 2006).

⁺ David Fromkin, *Europe's Last Summer: Who started the Great War in 1914?* (Vintage Books, New York, 2005), 3-14.

AFTERWORD

Just how has the Great War been remembered in the Maritimes? The mid-1920s witnessed the erection in towns and villages of many Great War monuments. Indeed, if one looks closely, almost all our war memorials originate from this time period. Tellingly, the names of the dead from the Second World War and the Korean War are added later, often in a manner which reveals that the original designers never envisioned having to add more names and new conflicts. Some of these monuments are truly impressive: bronze statues, situated prominently in public spaces in towns like Liverpool, Charlottetown, Chester, and St. Stephen.

By the late 1920s, however, times were changing, and there was a desire to move on. George Dow relates that, by then, when looking for a job, one did not admit to being a war veteran.* All veterans were regarded as unreliable drunks—a more poignant testament to the lack of adequate mental health services for returned soldiers need not be made. And so the veterans had to help themselves. They organized. First, there was the Great War Veterans Association founded in 1917, which in 1925 amalgamated with other groups and became the Canadian Legion of the British Empire Services League. The federal government was lobbied and some concessions and supports were won. Years passed and memories faded. New conflicts emerged (Ed Jay's prediction of another war proved sadly true). Many veterans disengaged from legion participation. Most did not speak about their experiences.

It is commonplace while speaking to the families of the men who penned these letters that the writers did not speak about the war. Some grandchildren visited homes where they were not even told that the picture of the handsome young man in uniform staring down at them was the granddad they were visiting! There are several possible explanations for this silence. First, to the returned victors goes the honour and privilege of moving on, of not dwelling in the past.

---

* Gene Dow, *World War One Reminiscences of a New Brunswick Veteran* (Fredericton, 1990), 3.

Secondly, there is the oft-repeated sentiment, found in the letters, that those at home, those who did not see, smell, and hear the reality, could not possibly comprehend or understand. Indeed, even those who did immediately experience the war often could not adequately process the events they witnessed. Fred Morell plainly states this belief and it is what lies behind Willie Muir's words to his mother, "It's awful, awful, awful."

A kilted Maritime soldier of the Great War: the Chester War Memorial.

PART FIVE : AFTERWORD

Finally, the difficulties of actually remembering have long been recognized. Oddly or tellingly, depending on one's perspective, one of the first and formative works of western civilization are the writings of an ancient Greek named Homer. He wrote sometime between 800 BC and 600 BC. His two famous works are the *Iliad* and the *Odyssey*. The *Iliad* is a war story and the *Odyssey* is the tale of a returning warrior. The *Iliad* is set towards the end of nine long years of conflict as the Greeks seek to capture and destroy the city of Troy. It is siege warfare, but Homer does not give us an ending. In his later book, the *Odyssey*, Homer tells us of a reunion banquet where two famous surviving veterans recall the events of those tragic years. The hostess is none other than Helen, Helen of Troy, the one man's wife. And this is the point. Helen serves the wine for the banquet. But Homer makes sure we are told that Helen, out of a special concern for the men, drugs the wine. The drug prevents the possibility of tears that day. They will recall the terrible battles and the loss of so many good friends, but they will be spared the emotional impact of their recollections. There will, for once, be memory without pain and recollection without regret. However, such relief, such release, is not within human power—the drug itself was a gift of the gods. On our own, Homer seems to say, mankind is left to contend with the scars of his own experience, the demons of his own creation. Perhaps then it will come as no surprise that it was another ancient Greek who first said that those who forget the past are fated to repeat its mistakes. On this anniversary of the Great War, may this reflection give another shade of meaning to the phrase "lest we forget."

BIOGRAPHICAL NOTATION ON LETTER WRITERS

Anderson, Waldo William, 709086. Born in McKees Mills, NB September 1898. Joined 104th Infantry Battalion at Sussex in autumn 1915. Wrote his parents and sister. Killed in action August 18, 1918.

Boehner, Frederick W., 283491. Born in West Lahave, NS, 1897. Joined 219th Infantry Battalion at Bridgewater in April 1916. Wrote his mother and father.

Bulmer, Howard Emerson, 832092. Born in Cherryfield, NB, 1893. Joined 145th Infantry Battalion at Moncton in January 1916. Wrote his brother Thomas.

Chapman, George T., 878225. Born in Glasgow, Scotland, lived in Sydney Mines, NS. Joined 185 Battalion, April 1916. Wrote his girlfriend, Mary, whom he later married.

Cook, Alfred R., 111110. Born in Halifax. Joined 6 Canadian Mounted Rifles, June 1915. Wrote his sister (Sarah), who was also Frederick Boehner's mother.

Drake, Arthur William, 1260329. Born in Cornwall, PEI, 1888. Joined 62 Battery in British Columbia in April 1916. Wrote his younger sister Charlotte.

Hape, William Kenneth, 222305. Born in Ecum Secum, NS, 1886. Joined 85th Battalion, Halifax in October 1915. Wrote his father. Killed in action April 5, 1918.

Harrison, Arthur Roy, 536309. Born in Gowland Mountain, NB, 1897. Joined No VIII O.S. Field Ambulance Unit (CAMC) at Sussex in August 1916. Wrote his mother, sister, and brother.

Heckbert, Harry, 3204333. Born in Summerside, PEI, 1887. Drafted March 23, 1918. Wrote his wife Iva Heckbert.

Jay, Edward Earl, 712735. Born in Fanning Brook, PEI, June 14, 1896. Joined 105 Battalion, May 1916. Wrote his mother and sister, Helen.

Kingston, Arthur Frederick, 1030674. Born in McAdam, NB, 1889. Joined 236th Overseas Battalion, The New Brunswick Kilties—Sir Sam's Own, April 1917. Wrote his sister, Mrs. Fred Pollock. Killed in action August 12, 1918.

Lawlor, Francis (Frank) John. Born in Newcastle, NB, 1893. Joined 132 Battalion. Wrote his mother, and sisters Clare and Annie. Killed in action April 7, 1918.

Lockhart, Frank Edwin. Born in Petitcodiac, NB, 1883. Joined New Brunswick's Fighting 26th Infantry Battalion in November 1914. Wrote his father, mother, and nursing sister, Ina. Killed in action April 6, 1916.

Lockhart, Ina. Born in Petitcodiac, NB, 1886. Graduate nurse of Newton Hospital Massachusetts. Served with the No. 22 (Harvard) General Hospital from December 1916 to June 1917 and in the Canadian Convalescent Hospital in Kent in late 1917 and 1918.

Loughery, George W., 445833. Born in Waterford, NB, 19 June 1896. Joined 55th Battalion October, 1915. Wrote his mother, Augusta Loughery, primarily, but also his sisters Saddie and Florence. Killed in action June 13, 1916.

McCann, Clarence Arthur, 90152. Born in Windsor, NS, 1891. Joined 28th Field Battery at Fredericton, March 1915. Wrote his parents Arthur and Ella McCann.

MacDonald, Duncan Chisholm, 1261434. Born in James River, NS, February 9, 1896. Joined No 5 Siege Battery CEF, June 1916. Wrote his father, mother, and sister Margaret.

McInnes, Charles, 817121. Born in Moncton, NB, July 7, 1880. Joined 140 Infantry Battalion at Sussex, November 1916. Wrote his wife, Bernice (nicknamed Niece), and his three daughters, Orlo, Margaret, and Mary.

Morell, Fred C., 335871. Born in Newcastle, NB, 1888. Joined 65

Overseas Battery, April 1916. Wrote his mother and wife.

Morell, Walter Horace, 335880. Born in Newcastle, NB, 1894. Joined 65 Overseas Battery, April 1916. Wrote his mother and wife, Hazel. Killed in action August 8, 1918.

Muir, William Alexander, 742647. Born in Mill Settlement, NB, 1897. Joined 115th Infantry Battalion, February, 1916 at Saint John. Transferred to 2nd Battalion Canadian Railroad Troops (CRT). Wrote his mother, Ethel (Mrs. David Muir).

Robinson, Arthur Clinton, 69813. Born in Tryon, PEI, 1896. Joined 26th Battalion at Saint John, NB, November 1914. Killed in action near St. Eloi, France, March 27, 1916. Wrote his aunt, Miss Carrie Robinson.

Smith, Leonard Ward, 470537. Born Boston, Massachusetts, USA, 1894. Joined 64 Infantry Battalion, 1915 at Sussex. Transferred to Canadian Machine Gun Corps (CMGC) August 1917. Wrote his father, mother, and younger sister (by four years), Dorothy.

SELECTED BIBLIOGRAPHY

GENERAL HISTORIES

Granatstein, J. L. *Hell's Corner: An Illustrated History of Canada in the First World War.* Vancouver: Douglas and McIntyre, 2004.

Keegan, John. *The First World War.* Toronto: Key Porter Books, 1998.

Morton, Desmond and J. L. Granatstein. *Marching to Armageddon: Canadians and the Great War 1914-1919.* Toronto: Lester and Orpen Dennys, 1989.

Terraine, John. *White Heat: The New Warfare 1914-18.* London: Guild Publishing, 1982.

Tuchman, Barbara. *The Guns of August.* New York: Presidio Press, 2004.

THE GREAT WAR'S LASTING EFFECTS

Eksteins, Modris. *Rites of Spring: The Great War and the Birth of the Modern Age.* Boston: Peter Davidson Books, 1989.

Fussell, Paul. *The Great War and Modern Memory.* New York: OUP, 1975.

Theobald, Andrew. *The Bitter Harvest of War: New Brunswick and the Conscription Crisis of 1917.* Fredericton: Goose Lane, 2008.

DIARIES, LETTERS, JOURNALS, AND RECOLLECTIONS BY CANADIANS

Adamson, Agar. *Letters of Agar Adamson 1914-1919.* Nepean: CEF Books, 1997.

Bain, J. Alexander. *A War Diary: A Canadian Signaller: My Experiences in the Great War:1914-1918*. Moncton: J. D. Bain, 1986.

Beatty, David Pierce. *Memories of the Forgotten War: The World War I Diary of Pte. V. E. Goodwin*. Saint John: Baie Verte Editions, 1988.

Becker, John H. *Silhouettes of The Great War*. Ottawa: CEF Books, 2001.

Bird, William R. *Ghosts Have Warm Hands*. Ottawa: CEF Books, 2002.

Brindle, Walter. *France & Flanders: Four Years Told in Poem & Story*. Saint John: J & A McMillan, 1919.

Dow, Gene. *World War One Reminiscences of a New Brunswick Veteran*. Fredericton: Centennial Printing, 1990.

Gaudet, Mary F. *From a Stretcher Handle: The World War I Journal and Poems of Pte. Frank Walker*. Charlottetown: Institute of Island Studies, 2000.

Peat, Harold R. *Private Peat*. New York: Grosset and Dunlap, 1917.

Pedley, James H. *Only This: A War Retrospective*. Ottawa: CEF Books, 1999.

Roy, Reginald S. *The Journal of Private Fraser*. Nepean: CEF Books, 1998.

Scott, Frederick G. *The Great War as I Saw It*. Ottawa: CEF Books, 2000.

Sguigna, Jen. *"Dear Mattie...". Letters from the First World War*. n.p., n.d.

Warner, Agnes. *My Beloved Poilus*. Saint John: Barnes and Co., 1917.

BATTALION (MARITIME) HISTORIES

Hayes, Joseph. *The Eighty-Fifth in France and Flanders*. Halifax: Royal Print & Litho, 1920.

MacDonald, F. B. and John J. Gardiner. *The Twenty-Fifth Battalion, Canadian Expeditionary Force: Nova Scotia's Famous Regiment in World War One*. Sydney: City Printers, 1983.

MacGowan, S. Douglas. *New Brunswick's "Fighting 26th": A History of the 26th New Brunswick Battalion, cef 1914-1919*. Saint John: Neptune Publishing, 1994.